T0321424

Collaborative Annotation for Reliable

Natural Language Processing

FOCUS SERIES

Series Editor Patrick Paroubek

Collaborative Annotation for Reliable Natural Language Processing

Technical and Sociological Aspects

Karën Fort

WILEY

First published 2016 in Great Britain and the United States by ISTE Ltd and John Wiley & Sons, Inc.

ISTE Ltd
27-37 St George's Road
London SW19 4EU
UK

www.iste.co.uk

John Wiley & Sons, Inc.
111 River Street
Hoboken, NJ 07030
USA

www.wiley.com

Library of Congress Control Number: 2016936602

British Library Cataloguing-in-Publication Data
A CIP record for this book is available from the British Library
ISSN 2051-2481 (Print)
ISSN 2051-249X (Online)
ISBN 978-1-84821-904-5

Contents

Preface

This book presents a unique opportunity for me to construct what I hope to be a consistent image of collaborative manual annotation for Natural Language Processing (NLP). I partly rely on work that has already been published elsewhere, with some of it only in French, most of it in reduced versions and all of it available on my personal website.[1] Whenever possible, the original article should be cited in preference to this book.

Also, I refer to publications in French. I retained these publications because there was no equivalent one in English, hoping that at least some readers will be able to understand them.

This work owes a lot to my interactions with Adeline Nazarenko (LIPN/University of Paris 13) both during and after my PhD thesis. In addition, it would not have been conducted to its end without (a lot of) support and help from Benoît Habert (ICAR/ENS of Lyon).

Finally, I would like to thank all the friends who supported me in writing this book and proofread parts of it, as well as the colleagues who kindly accepted that their figures be part of it.

---

1 Here: http://karenfort.org/Publications.php.

List of Acronyms

ACE   Automatic Content Extraction

ACK   Annotation Collection Toolkit

ACL   Association for Computational Linguistics

AGTK   Annotation Graph Toolkit

API   Application Programming Interface

ATALA   *Association pour le Traitement Automatique des LAngues* (French Computational Linguistics Society)

HIT   `Amazon Mechanical Turk` **Human Intelligence Task**

LDC   Linguistic Data Consortium

NLP   Natural Language Processing

POS   Part-Of-Speech

Introduction

I.1. Natural Language Processing and manual annotation: Dr Jekyll and Mr Hy|ide?

I.1.1. *Where linguistics hides*

Natural Language Processing (NLP) has witnessed two major evolutions in the past 25 years: first, the extraordinary success of machine learning, which is now, for better or for worse (for an enlightening analysis of the phenomenon see [CHU 11]), overwhelmingly dominant in the field, and second, the multiplication of evaluation campaigns or shared tasks. Both involve manually annotated corpora, for the training and evaluation of the systems (see Figure I.1).

These corpora progressively became the hidden pillars of our domain, providing food for our hungry machine learning algorithms and reference for evaluation. Annotation is now the place where linguistics hides in NLP.

However, manual annotation has largely been ignored for quite a while, and it took some time even for annotation guidelines to be recognized as essential [NÉD 06]. When the performance of the systems began to stall, manual annotation finally started to generate some interest in the community, as a potential leverage for improving the obtained results [HOV 10, PUS 12].

This is all the more important, as it was proven that systems trained on badly annotated corpora underperform. In particular, they tend to reproduce annotation errors when these errors follow a regular pattern and do not correspond to simple noise [REI 08]. Furthermore, the quality of manual annotation is crucial when it is used to evaluate NLP systems. For example, an inconsistently annotated reference corpus would undoubtedly favor machine learning systems, therefore prejudicing rule-based systems in evaluation campaigns. Finally, the quality of linguistic analyses would suffer from an annotated corpus that is unreliable.

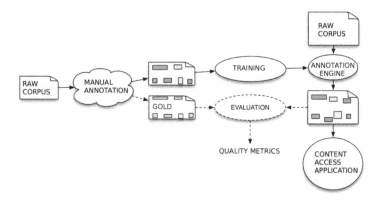

Figure I.1. *Manually annotated corpora and machine learning process*

Although some efforts have been made lately to address some of the issues presented by manual annotation, there is still little research done on the subject. This book aims at providing some (hopefully useful) insights into the subject. It is partly based on a PhD thesis [FOR 12a] and on some published articles, most of them written in French.

I.1.2. *What is annotation?*

The renowned British corpus linguist Geoffrey Leech [LEE 97] defines corpus annotation as: "The practice of adding interpretative, linguistic information to an electronic corpus of spoken and/or written language data. 'Annotation' can also refer to the end-product of this process". This definition highlights the interpretative dimension of annotation but limits it to "linguistic information" and to some specific sources, without mentioning its goal.

In [HAB 05], Benoît Habert extends Leech's definition, first, by not restricting the type of added information: "annotation consists of adding information (a stabilized interpretation) to language data: sounds, characters and gestures".[1] He adds that "it associates two or three steps: (i) segmentation to delimit fragments of data and/or add specific points; (ii) grouping of segments or points to assign them a category; (iii) (potentially) creating relations between fragments or points".[2]

We build on these and provide a wider definition of annotation:

DEFINITION (Annotation).– *Annotation covers both the process of adding a note on a source signal and the whole set of notes or each note that results from this process, without a* priori *presuming what the nature of the source (text, video, images, etc.), the semantic content of the note (numbered note, value chosen in a reference list or free text), its position (global*

---

1 In French, the original version is: "l'annotation consiste à ajouter de l'information (une interprétation stabilisée) aux données langagières : sons, caractères et gestes".
2 In French: "[e]lle associe deux ou trois volets: (i) segmentation pour délimiter des fragments de données et/ou ajout de points singuliers; (ii) regroupement de segments ou de points pour leur affecter une catégorie; (iii) (éventuellement) mise en relation de fragments ou de points".

or local) or its objective (evaluation, characterization and simple comment) are.

Basically, annotating is adding a *note* to a *source signal*. The annotation is therefore the note, *anchored* in one point or in a segment of the source signal (see Figure I.2). In some cases, the span can be the whole document (for example, in indexing).

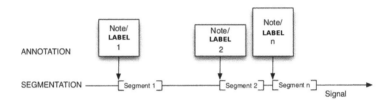

Figure I.2. *Anchoring of notes in the source signal*

In the case of relations, two or more segments of the source signal are connected and a note is added to the connection. Often, a note is added to the segments too.

This definition of annotation includes many NLP applications, from transcription (the annotation of speech with its written interpretation) to machine translation (the annotation of one language with its translation in another language). However, the analysis we conduct here is mostly centered on categorization (adding a category taken from a list to a segment of signal or between segments of signal). It does not mean that it does not apply to transcription, for example, but we have not yet covered this thoroughly enough to be able to say that the research detailed in this book can directly apply to such applications.

In NLP, annotations can either be added manually by a human interpreter or automatically by an analysis tool. In the first case, the interpretation can reflect parts of the subjectivity of its authors. In the second case, the interpretation is entirely determined by the knowledge and the algorithm integrated in the tool. We are focusing here on manual annotation as a task executed by human agents whom we call annotators.

I.1.3. *New forms, old issues*

Identifying the first evidence of annotation in history is impossible, but it seems likely that it appeared in the first writings on a physical support allowing for a text to be easily commented upon.

Annotations were used for private purposes (comments from readers) or public usage (explanations from professional readers). They were also used for communicating between writers (authors or copyists, i.e. professional readers) [BAK 10]. In these latter senses, the annotations had a collaborative dimension.

Early manuscripts contained *glosses*, i.e. according to the online Merriam-Webster dictionary:[3] "a brief explanation (as in the margin or between the lines of a text) of a difficult or obscure word or expression". Glosses were used to inform and train the reader. Other types of annotations were used, for example to update the text (*apostils*). The form of glosses could vary considerably and [MUZ 85, p. 134] distinguishes between nine different types. *Interlinear glosses* appear between the lines of a manuscript, *marginal glosses* in the margin, *surrounding glosses* in the circumference and *separating glosses* between the explained paragraphs. They are more or less merged into the text, from the *organic gloss*, which can be considered as part of the text, to the *formal gloss*, which constitutes a text in itself, transmitted from copy to copy (as today's standoff annotations).[4]

---

3 See 3.1 in http://www.merriam-webster.com/dictionary/gloss.

4 For more information and illustrations on the subject, see: http://codicologia.irht.cnrs.fr.

Physical marks, like *indention square brackets*, could also be added to the text (see an example in a text by Virgil[5] in Figure I.3), indicating the first commented words. Interestingly, this primitive anchoring did not indicate the end of the commented part.

Siciliæ:qd nunc Megara dr ul'loc⁹ iattica ubi   Hybla
optimū mel nafcit & pofuit fpēm pro genere.
Depafta flore. depaftū flore hñs. Salicti:
uirgulti genus eo ꝗ falit & furgit cito.Salictū   Salictū
ubi funt multæ falices. Sæpe fufurro leui dul
ci murmur hic uocat rufticū ad dulcia ꝗ fūt in
reb⁹ quibus delectat. Sōnū inire.i. dormire.
Frōdator.i.ruftic⁹ uel aial qd frōdib⁹ uefcit
Nā tria gñ a fūt frōdatog. Frōdator q arbo   Fronda
res āputat & frōdibus manipulos facit hyemis   tor
tpe aialib⁹ ad paftū offerēdos:& q manibus ui
tiū folia auellit quo ardor folis uuā maturiore
reddat:aut auis ꝗi frōdib⁹ hitat: & his uefcit:
uel et palūbes ꝗi frōdib⁹ nidificant. Ad auras
i.idie. Raucæ.βραγχ1λθθ.i.brūgidæPalū
bes colūbe:ꝗs uulg⁹ tetas uocat & ñ dr latine:
fed multorū auctoritas latinum facit. Cicero
i elegia ꝗ thalemaftis fcribit. lā mar tyrrhenū   Gemer
lōge pēitufꝯ palūbes.Reliqt. Gemer:cāere:

Figure I.3. *Indention square brackets in a text by Virgil. Bibliothèque municipale de Lyon (Courtesy of Town Library of Lyon), France, Res. 104 950*

The same limitation applies to the *auctoritates*, which appeared in the 8th Century to cite the authors (considered as authorities) of a citation. The anchoring of the annotation is noted by two dots above the first word of the citation, without indicating the end of it (see Figure I.4).

---

5 Opera, com. de Servius. Milan: Leonardo Pachel, 1509, in-fol., source: http://enssibal.enssib.fr/bibliotheque/documents/travaux/sordet/nav.liv.ancien. html

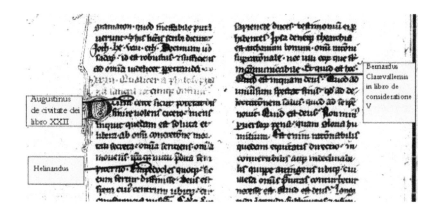

Figure I.4. *Anchoring of* auctoritates *in* De sancta Trinitate, *Basel, UB B.IX.5, extracted from [FRU 12], by courtesy of the authors*

This delimitation problem was accentuated by the errors made by the copyists, who moved the *auctoritates* and their anchors. To solve this issue, and without the possibility of using other markers like quotes (which will appear much later), introductory texts (pre- and peri-annotation) were invented.

From the content point of view, the evolution went from the *explanatory gloss* (free text) to the citation of authors (name of the author, from a limited list of authorities), precisely identified in the text. As for the anchoring, it improved progressively to look like our present text markup.

This rapid overview shows that many of today's preoccupations – frontiers to delimit, annotations chosen freely or from a limited reference, anchoring, metadata to transmit – have been around for a while. It also illustrates the fact that adding an annotation is not a spontaneous gesture, but one which is reflected upon, studied, a gesture which is learned.

I.2. Rediscovering annotation

I.2.1. *A rise in diversity and complexity*

A good indicator of the rise in annotation diversity and complexity is the annotation language. The annotation language is the vocabulary used to annotate the flow of data. In a lot of annotation cases in NLP, this language is constrained.[6] It can be of various types.

The simplest is the Boolean type. It covers annotation cases in which only one category is needed. A segment is annotated with this category (which can only be implicit) or not annotated at all. Experiences like the identification of obsolescence segments in encyclopaedia [LAI 09] use this type of language.

Then come the first-order languages. Type languages are, for example, used for morpho-syntactic annotation without features (part-of-speech) or with features (morpho-syntax). The first case is in fact rather rare, as even if the tagset seems little structured, as in the *Penn Treebank* [SAN 90], features can almost always be deduced from it (for example, *NNP*, proper name singular, and *NNPS*, proper name plural, could be translated into *NNP* + *Sg* and *NNP* + *Pl*).

As for relations, a large variety are annotated in NLP today, from binary-oriented relations (for example, gene renaming relations [JOU 11]) to unoriented n-ary relations (for example, co-reference chains as presented in [POE 05]).

Finally, second-order languages could be used, for example, to annotate relations on relations. In the soccer domain, for example, *intercept(pass(p1, p2), p3)* represents a pass (relation) between two players (p1 and p2), which is

---

6 Note that this is not the case for transcription or machine translation, which both need unconstrained annotation languages (the natural language itself).

intercepted by another player (p3). In practice, we simplify the annotation by adapting it to a first-order language by reifying the first relation [FOR 12b]. This is so commonly done that we are aware of no example of annotation using a second-order language.

Jean Véronis concluded his state-of-the-art of the automatic annotation technology in 2000 with a figure summarizing the situation [VÉR 00]. On this figure, only the part-of-speech annotation and the multilingual alignment of sentences are considered "operational". Most applications are considered as prototypes (prosody, partial syntax, multilingual words alignment), and the rest were still not allowing for "applications which are useful in real situations" (full syntax, discourse semantics) or were close to prototypes (phonetic transcription, lexical semantics). The domain has quickly evolved, and today much more complex annotations can be performed on different media and related to a large variety of phenomena.

In the past few years, we have witnessed the multiplication of annotation projects involving video sources, in particular sign language videos. A workshop on the subject (DEGELS) took place during the French NLP conference (TALN) in 2011 and 2012,[7] and a training concerning video corpus annotation was organized by the Association pour le Traitement Automatique des LAngues (ATALA) in 2011.[8]

Moreover, more and more complex semantic annotations are now carried out on a regular basis, like opinions or sentiment annotation. In the biomedical domain, proteins and gene names annotation is now completed by the annotation of relations like gene renaming [JOU 11] or relations between entities, in particular within the

---

7 See: http://degels.limsi.fr/.
8 See: http://tals.limsi.fr/jatala2011.html.

framework of BioNLP shared tasks.[9] Semantic annotations are also performed using a formal model (i.e. an ontology) [CIM 03], and linked data are now used to annotate corpora, like during the Biomedical Linked Annotation Hackathon (BLAH).[10]

Finally, annotations that are now considered as traditional, like named entities or anaphora, are getting significantly more complex, for example with added structuring [GRO 11].

However, there are still few corpora freely available with different levels of annotations, including with annotations from different linguistic theories. *MASC (Manually Annotated Sub-Corpus)* [IDE 08][11] is an interesting exception, as it includes, among others, annotations of frames *à la* FrameNet [BAK 98] and senses *à la* WordNet [FEL 98]. Besides, we are not aware of any freely available multimedia-annotated corpus with each level of annotation aligned to the source, but it should not be long until it is developed.

The ever-growing complexity of annotation is taken into account in new annotation formats, like GrAF [IDE 07]; however, it still has to be integrated in the methodology and in the preparation of an annotation campaign.

I.2.2. *Redefining manual annotation costs*

The exact cost of an annotation campaign is rarely mentioned in research papers. One noteworthy exception is the *Prague Dependency TreeBank*, for which the authors of [BÖH 01] announce a cost of US$600,000. Other articles detail the number of persons involved in the project they present: *GENIA* for example, involved 5 part-time

---

9 See the 2016 shared tasks here: http://2016.bionlp-st.org/.

10 See: http://2015.linkedannotation.org/.

11 See here: http://www.anc.org/data/masc/corpus/.

annotators, a senior coordinator and one junior coordinator for 1.5 year [KIM 08]. Anyone who participated in such a project knows it that manual annotation is very costly.

However, the resulting annotated corpora, when they are well-documented and available in a suitable format, as shown in [COH 05], are used well beyond and long after the training of the original model or the original research purpose. A typical example of this is the *Penn TreeBank* corpus, created in the beginning of the 90s [MAR 93] and that is still used more than 20 years later (it is easy to find recent research like [BOH 13]). On the contrary, the tools trained on these corpora usually become quickly outdated as research is making progress. An interesting example is that of the once successful PARTS tagger, created using the *Brown* corpus [CHU 88] and used to pre-annotate the *Penn TreeBank*. However, when the technology becomes mature and generates results that the users consider satisfactory, the lifespan of such tools gets longer. This is the case for example in part-of-speech tagging for the TreeTagger [SCH 97], which, with nearly 96% of accuracy for French [ALL 08], is still widely used, despite the fact that it is now less efficient then state-of-the-art results (MElt [DEN 09] for example, obtains 98% accuracy on French). Such domains are still rare.

This trivial remark concerning the lifetime of corpora leads to important consequences with regard to the way we build manually annotated corpora.

First, it puts the cost of the manual work into perspective: a manual corpus costing US$600,000 like the *Prague Dependency TreeBank*, that has been used for more than 20 years like the *Penn TreeBank* is not that expensive (US$30,000 per year). It is even cheaper if you consider the total number of projects which used it: a quick search in the

Association for Computational Linguistics (ACL) anthology[12] with the keyword "Penn TreeBank" reveals that more than 30 research articles directly use the corpus (including the *Penn Discourse TreeBank*, but excluding the Penn treebanks created for other languages like Chinese), which corresponds to US$20,000 per project. If we consider that many research projects used it without putting its name in the title of the article, like the paper we wrote on the effects of pre-annotation [FOR 10], we can assume that a lot more than 30 projects were based on the *Penn TreeBank*, lowering its cost to probably less than that of a long internship.

Second, it is a strong argument not for building manually annotated corpora according to the possibilities of the system(s) that will use it, as they will be long forgotten when the annotated corpus is still be used. If the corpus is too dependent on the systems' (limited) capabilities, it will not be useful anymore when the algorithms become more efficient.

Third, this implies that manual annotation should be of high quality, i.e. well-prepared, well-documented and regularly evaluated with adequate metrics. Manual annotation campaign preparation is often rushed and overlooked, because people want to get it over with as quickly as possible.[13] This has been particularly emphasized in [SAM 00], where the author notes (on p. 7) that: "[...] it seems to me that natural language computing has yet to take on board the software-engineering lesson of the primacy of problem analysis and documentation over coding".

There is, in fact, a need for annotation engineering procedures and tools and this is what this book aims at providing, at least partly.

---

12 See: http://aclanthology.info/.

13 Obviously, there are still people who consider it trivial to annotate manually. They usually change their mind quickly when they start doing it for real.

Annotating Collaboratively

1.1. The annotation process (re)visited

A simplified representation of the annotation process is shown in Figure 1.4. We will detail further in this section the different steps of this process, but we first introduce a theoretical view on the consensus and show how limited the state of the art on the subject is.

1.1.1. *Building consensus*

The central question when dealing with manual corpus annotation is how to obtain reliable annotations, that are both useful (i.e. meaningful) and consistent. In order to achieve this and to solve the "annotation conundrum" [LIB 09], we have to understand the annotation process. As we saw in section I.1.2, annotating consists of identifying the segment(s) to annotate and adding a note (also called a label or a tag) to it or them. In some annotation tasks, segments can be linked by a relation, oriented or not, and the note applies to this relation. In most cases, the note is in fact a category, taken from a list (the tagset).

Alain Desrosières, a famous French statistician, worked on the building of the French socio-professional categories

[DES 02] and wrote a number of books on categorization (among which, translated into English, [DES 98]). His work is especially relevant to our subject, as he precisely analyzed what categorizing means.

First, and this is fundamental for the annotation process, he makes a clear distinction between *measuring* and *quantifying* [DES 14]. Measuring "implies that something already exists under a form that is measurable, according to a realistic metrology, like the height of the Mont Blanc".[1] Quantifying, on the other hand, consists of "expressing and transforming into a numerical form what used to be expressed with words and not numbers".[2] For this to be realized, a series of conventions of equivalence should be elaborated through collaboration.

The categories are not measurable, they have to be agreed upon before they can be applied. There has to be a consensus on them and one piece of evidence that the categories emerge from a consensus (and are not "natural") is that they can change in time. A typical example of this are named entities, which evolved from proper names only [COA 92] to the MUC (Message Understanding Conferences) classic categories (*person, location, organization*) [GRI 96] and on to structured named entities, with subtypes and components [GRO 11]. This evolution was initiated and validated by the named entity recognition community. This also happened, although in a less spectacular way, with parts-of-speech [COL 88].

The result of this consensus-building process is logged in the annotation guidelines, that are used by the annotators to decide what to annotate (which segment(s)) and how (with

---

1 In French: "[...] l'idée de mesure [...] implique que quelque chose existe *déjà* sous une forme mesurable selon une métrologie réaliste, comme la hauteur du Mont Blanc".

2 In French: "exprimer et faire exister sous une forme numérique ce qui auparavant, était exprimé par des mots et non par des nombres."

which category). However, even with very detailed guidelines, like the 80 pages long *Quæro* structured named entity annotation guidelines,[3] the annotators will still disagree on some annotations. This is why we need constant evaluation (to see when they disagree) and consensus building (to improve the consistency of annotations).

Once this is posited, there remain many practical issues: who should participate in the annotation guidelines? and how can we determine when they are ready, or at least ready-enough to start annotating? When do we start evaluating the agreement between annotators, and how? The following sections will hopefully provide answers to these questions.[4]

1.1.2. *Existing methodologies*

Manual annotation has long been considered as straightforward in linguistics and NLP. Some researchers still consider that computing inter-annotator agreement is useless (since the annotators *have to* agree) and it took some time and demonstration [NÉD 06] before the need for an annotation guide became obvious. It is therefore logical that the interest for the manual annotation process itself is growing slowly.

If speech processing inspired the evaluation trend and metrics like inter-annotator agreements, corpus linguistics provided good practices for manual annotation, in particular with Geoffrey Leech's seven maxims [LEE 93] and later work on annotation [LEE 97], and with collective efforts like [WYN 05]. However, it did not propose any in-depth analysis of the annotation process itself.

---

3 Available here: http://www.quaero.org/media/files/bibliographie/quaero-guide-annotation-2011.pdf.

4 The sections about the annotation process, from preparation to finalization, are adapted from my PhD thesis (in French) [FOR 12a].

Some high-level analyses of the work of the annotators were carried out, for example to create the *UniProt* Standard Operating Procedures[5] or the GATE manual.[6] However, very few studies are concerned with the manual annotation process as a whole.

According to Geoffrey Sampson [SAM 00], the "problem analysis and documentation" of annotation should be taken much more seriously and be considered primary over coding (annotating). His reflection is based on a parallel with software development and engineering. Interestingly, this parallel has been extended to the annotation methodology with "agile corpus creation" and "agile annotation" [VOO 08], an analogy with agile development [BEC 11].

From our point of view, the methodology presented in [BON 05], even if it is generally not cited as a reference for agile annotation, pioneered the field. The authors show that computing inter-annotator agreement very early in the campaign allows them to identify problems rapidly and to update the annotation guide accordingly, in order to minimize their impact.

Agile annotation [VOO 08] goes further as it reorganizes completely the traditional phases of manual annotation (see Figure 1.1) for a more lenient process, with several cycles of annotation/guideline update. To our knowledge, this methodology was used only once in a real annotation project [ALE 10]. Therefore, it is difficult to understand to what extent it really differs from the methodology presented in [BON 05] and whether it will produce better results.

---

5 See: http://www.uniprot.org/help/manual_curation and http://geneontology.org/page/go-annotation-standard-operating-procedures.
6 See: https://gate.ac.uk/teamware/man-ann-intro.pdf.

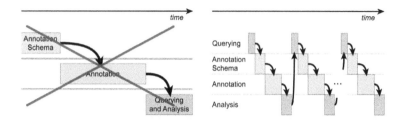

Figure 1.1. *Traditional annotation phases (on the left) and cycles of agile annotation (on the right). Reproduction of Figure 2 from [VOO 08], by courtesy of the authors*

Eduard Hovy presented a tutorial on manual annotation during the ACL 2010 conference in which he gave interesting insights about methodology and process. This partial methodology is detailed in [HOV 10] and shown in Figure 1.2. It includes the training and evaluation of the system (*engine*), the results of which can lead to modification of the manual annotation. Our point of view on this is quite different and we have already expressed it in section I.2.2: manual annotation should be carried out with an application in mind, not in accordance with a tool, as (i) it would largely bias any evaluation performed with the annotated corpus and (ii) would limit the lifespan of the corpus. However, the manual annotation part of this methodology is the most complete we know of. It includes six steps: (1) building the corpus, (2) developing the tagset and writing a first version of the guidelines, (3) annotating a sample of the corpus, (4) comparing the annotators' decisions, (5) measuring the inter-annotator agreement and determining which level of agreement would be satisfactory (if not, return to step 2), (6) annotating the corpus. Although it includes a pre-campaign (steps 2 to 5), post-campaign (delivery and maintenance) and consensus building elements (meetings), it neither defines who does what (the precise roles), nor gives indicators in order to move up one step, particularly concerning the training of the annotators.

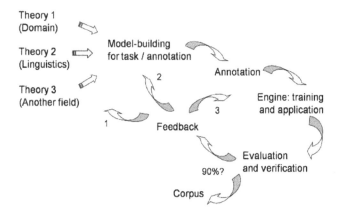

Figure 1.2. *Generic annotation pipeline (Figure 1 from [HOV 10], by courtesy of the authors)*

The book written by James Pustejovsky and Amber Stubbs [PUS 12] also presents a view on annotation where the training of systems and the manual process interpenetrate. This is the MATTER methodology (for *Model-Annotate-Train-Test-Evaluate-Revise*). Within MATTER lies the manual annotation cycle itself, MAMA (for *Model-Annotate-Model-Annotate*). In this, annotation is further decomposed into another cycle: Model and Guidelines-Annotate-Evaluate-Revise. According to MAMA, the corpus is entirely annotated by at least two annotators, several times, then completely adjudicated by an expert. This is ideal, but very costly if not done with crowdsourcing. Another weak point in this methodology is that it contains various cycles and does not indicate when they should be stopped.

We will focus here on the annotation process and will not detail the corpus creation, although it is a very important step. Useful information on the subject can be found in [PUS 12], but we advise reading John Sinclair first, in particular the easily accessible [SIN 05].

We have participated in a dozen annotation campaigns (in half of them, as campaign manager), most of them within the framework of the *Quæro* project. These campaigns cover a wide range of annotation types (and were carried out either in French or in English): POS, dependency syntax, named entities, gene renaming relations, protein and gene names, football, pharmacology. They allowed us to build and test the annotation process framework we propose in the following sections.

1.1.3. *Preparatory work*

An annotation campaign does not start with the annotation itself. It requires some preparatory work to identify the actors, to get to know the corpus and to write a first version of the guidelines. This should not be neglected, as the productivity and quality of the annotation largely depend on it.

1.1.3.1. *Identifying the actors*

The following reflection was started with Sophie Rosset (LIMSI-CNRS). It aims at identifying clearly the various actors in an annotation campaign and showing the tensions that can emerge from their often diverging visions of the campaign.

Our experience and the state-of-the-art allow us to distinguish between seven main roles in an annotation campaign:

1) final users: users of the potential application developed using the annotated corpus;

2) financier(s): person(s) representing the organism(s) funding the campaign (often funding agencies);

3) client(s): person(s) or team(s) who need the corpus to train, create or evaluate their system;

4) campaign manager: person in charge of planning the campaign and guaranteeing its performance. In general,

the manager is the contact person between the client, the evaluators and the experts (and in some rarer cases the financiers);

5) expert annotators: annotators who are specialized in the domain of the corpus (sometimes in the annotation domain), who select the annotators, train them, evaluate them, answer their questions and adjudicate the annotation when necessary;

6) annotators: persons performing the biggest part of the annotation; in crowdsourcing annotation they are sometimes called "non-experts", but we will see in the next chapter that this is far from the reality;

7) evaluator(s): person(s) in charge of evaluating the quality of the annotated corpus and/or of the systems trained or evaluated with this corpus.

All these roles are not always fulfilled in an annotation campaign. For example, evaluators can be absent from smaller internal campaigns, with no external evaluation. As for the number of actors per role, it can vary, but the annotation manager should be a unique person, in order to avoid inconsistencies in the campaign. As for experts, there should be at least two to build a mini-reference, so if the manager is an expert, there has to be another one. Finally, we will see in section 1.4 that to evaluate the quality of the annotation, at least two annotators are needed. In the meta study presented in [BAY 11], the authors concluded by the suggestion to use at least five annotators for the most difficult tasks, and at least three or four annotators for other tasks. Previously, it was shown in [KLE 09] that the use of more annotators enabled us to lower the influence of chance on the inter-annotator agreement results. However, it was demonstrated in [BHA 10] that well-trained annotators produce better annotations than a "crowd of non-experts". As we will see further, the number of annotators is not the key, but training is.

Obviously, all the roles we presented here should not necessarily be perfectly distinct and organized as a hierarchy in all campaigns, but when they are missing or merged with another role, it should be taken into account, since it may generate biases. For example, the financier, being in the most powerful position, could bias the whole campaign. Therefore, he/she should not intervene directly on the annotators or the annotation guide. Futhermore, when the financier is not the client, the balance of the campaign is more sound. With no financier, the client has a lot of influence (maybe too much). As for the manager, he/she is accountable for the overall balance of the campaign and should not play any other role. If he/she is also an expert (which is often the case), he/she has to work with other experts to compensate this imbalance. Finally, the expert has not only to supervise the annotators, but also to be their representative. It should be noted that, although the annotator is at the bottom of this organization, he/she is at the center of the annotation, as the value added to the corpus is the interpretation provided by the annotators. It is therefore essential to take their remarks and suggestions into account. Annotators on microworking platforms like Amazon Mechanical Turk are paid by the task and have no interest in giving feedback to the *Requester* (and the platform does not encourage them to do so), their point of view is therefore seldom considered.

Finally, we would like here to nuance a common statement according to which the researchers, who are often both managers of the campaign and experts of the annotation task, are the best annotators. Our experience shows that (i) even if they are experts of the task, they are not necessarily experts of the domain and can experience difficulties understanding the context, like in the case of named entity annotation in old press (what was "Macé" in "krach Macé"? A person? An organization? A place?) and (ii) they too often question the annotation guide they wrote or they do not consult it enough. During the structured named entity annotation campaign in broadcast news, the four experts (researchers) who annotated the mini-reference obtained inter-agreement scores which were not better than that of the annotators.

1.1.3.2. *Taking the corpus into account*

We managed a football annotation campaign in which the heterogeneity of the corpus affected all the aspects of the campaign: the selection of a sub-corpus for the training of the annotators, the length of the training, the complexity of the annotation scheme and the resulting annotation quality. Based on this experience, we showed in [FOR 11b] how important it is to have an in-depth knowledge of the corpus to annotate.

This is all the more true as the campaign manager does not necessarily choose the corpus on which the annotation will be performed, he/she therefore has to adapt the campaign to the specificities of the source. This means that the corpus should be analyzed and decomposed into its constituents: domains, sources, media, etc.

The best way to "dive into" the corpus is to annotate a small but representative part of it, even before starting the campaign. Obviously, this is possible only if the domain and the language are mastered by the manager. If not, he/she should use one or several experts to help with this work.

This is what we did in several annotation campaigns, as campaign manager [FOR 11b] or as advisor [ROS 12]. It allowed us not only to identify problems with the annotation guide even before the annotators started working, but also to create a pre-reference for evaluation. In some cases, having the client annotate this pre-reference is a good way to validate the choices that were made and to check that the annotation is not diverging too much from the initial application.

Whether it is done *a priori*, during the corpus selection, or *a posteriori*, once the corpus is selected, a precise analysis of its contents and of the consequences of this on the campaign has to be performed as soon as possible.

1.1.3.3. *Creating and modifying the annotation guide*

The annotation guide (also called annotation guidelines) is now recognized as essential to an annotation campaign. For the structured named entity annotation campaign, the design of the annotation guide took six months. This preparatory work was costly (especially as it involved several researchers), even if the resulting guide has been used in a second annotation campaign, as well as for another French project (ETAPE).

However, writing an annotation guide is not a one-shot task performed at the beginning of a campaign, with only a couple of modifications added afterwards. On the contrary, the guide evolves during a large part of the annotation campaign. It is the necessary condition for its usability as the accompanying documentation for the resulting annotated corpus.

However, a first version of the guide should be written rapidly, before the campaign starts, in collaboration with the client (we call this a pre-reference). It is then tested by annotating a mini-reference. Usually, this generates a first round of modifications. During the break-in phase, the document will continue to be improved, thanks to the feedback from the annotators. In turn, these modifications should allow for a better quality of the annotation and for a gain in time, since the ill-defined or ill-understood categories and rules generate a waste of time for the annotators. Several cycles annotation/revision of the guide can be necessary to obtain a certain stability, which is demonstrated through a constant and sufficient annotation quality.

If their underlying principles are very close, agile annotation [VOO 08, ALE 10] differs from the methodology proposed in [BON 05] in that the cycles continue until the very end of the campaign (see Figure 1.1). However, it seems to us that when the annotation is stabilized in terms of annotation quality and speed, it is not necessary to go on with the process, even if other evaluations should be performed to ensure non-regression.

Finally, ill-defined or ill-understood categories are a cause of stress and mistakes. In order to alleviate the stress and to keep a precise trace of the problems encountered during annotation, it is important to offer the annotators the possibility to add an uncertainty note when they have doubts about their decisions. This uncertainty note can take the form of typed features (for example, see Figure 1.10: uncertainty-type="too generic"), which allow for an easier processing. These types of uncertainties should of course be described in the annotation guide.

We give a number of recommendations concerning the annotation guide in [FOR 09]. We briefly summarize them here:

– indicate *what* should be annotated rather than *how*;

– do not *a priori* exclude what would be doubtful or too difficult to reproduce with a NLP system;

– give the annotators a clear vision of the application in view;

– add precise definitions, justify the methodological choices and explain the underlying logics of the annotation (do not just provide examples).

Following these recommendations should empower and motivate the annotators, by giving them access to the underlying logics. This way, we allow them to evolve from a "father-son" relationship to a pair relationship [AKR 91], which influences the annotation quality and is all the more necessary if the annotators are (corpus) domain experts who have to be as autonomous as possible.

It is therefore essential not to describe everything and to leave a sufficient interpretation margin to the annotators so that they can really add value to the corpus. Guidelines which are too detailed and long to consult are less useful than a condensed guide, presenting what is essential, with a few well-chosen examples and concrete tests to distinguish between the categories which are known to be ambiguous. From this point of view, the *Penn Treebank* guidelines for POS annotation are an example to follow.

In crowdsourcing, this principle is pushed to its maximum, as the annotation guide is reduced to a couple of lines on `Amazon Mechanical Turk`, or to a couple of pages for a gamified interface like `Phrase Detectives`. In these cases, the annotation task should remain simple or the training should replace at least part of the guidelines.

The preparatory work allows us to clearly define the application in view, to write a first version of the annotation guide, to explore the corpus and to identify the actors of the campaign. It includes three main phases: (i) the pre-campaign, during which a mini-reference is agreed upon and the annotators are trained, (ii) the annotation itself, which starts with a break-in period and includes regular evaluations and updates, and (iii) finalization, which consists of a manual or automatized correction of the annotated corpus, before its publication. The general organization of an annotation campaign is shown in Figure 1.4.

1.1.4. *Pre-campaign*

The consensus building phase is too often reduced to a couple of meetings, when it should be an iterative process that involves various actors. If the pre-campaign is organized by the campaign manager, he/she is generally associated with (annotation) domain experts in building the corpus sample which will be annotated to be used as a mini-reference.

He/she is also in charge of the training of the annotators, during which they will give the first feedback on the campaign (organization, tools, guidelines).

1.1.4.1. *Building the mini-reference*

Building a mini-reference from the very beginning of the campaign (see Figure 1.4) presents numerous advantages. First, it allows us to test in real conditions the first version of the annotation guide, written by the manager, sometimes in collaboration with the client. Building the mini-reference also allows us to evaluate the reliability of the annotation very early in the campaign. The result of this evaluation will be compared to others, later in the campaign. Moreover, once it is finalized, the mini-reference contains all the information needed to compute the complexity dimensions of the campaign (see section 1.2), that will give precise indications to select the most appropriate tools for the campaign, be they annotation tools (see section 1.3), pre-annotation tools or methodological solutions (for example adding elements to the guidelines). This step also allows us to select the most appropriate inter-annotator agreement metric (see section 1.4).

The reference sub-corpus (or mini-reference) is a sample from the original "raw" corpus, if possible representative. The preparatory work (see section 1.1.3) allowed us to establish a detailed typology of the corpus and the creation of a representative sub-corpus for the mini-reference can be done by selecting files (or parts of files) corresponding to each identified type, in a proportionate way. Our goal here is not to be perfectly representative (which is an illusion anyway), but to cover enough phenomena to deal with a maximum of issues during the annotation of the mini-reference.

The size of this sub-corpus mostly depends on the time available for this annotation, but a corpus that is too small or an insufficient representativeness can lead to important errors in the computation of the complexity dimensions of the campaign. For example, we noticed when we computed the complexity dimensions for the structured named entity annotation campaign, that the selected sample was too small. The theoretical ambiguity is relatively limited on the mini-reference (around 0.15) and much higher on the global corpus (around 0.4). These results are detailed in [FOR 12d].

This mini-reference is annotated by the campaign manager (or by an expert, if the domain of the corpus is unknown to the manager), with at least one expert. The annotation phase is punctuated by informal meetings during which modifications of the tagset and of the guidelines are decided upon. Collective solutions are found to disagreements by consensus. We created mini-references for two annotation campaigns (football and structured named entities) and in both cases they were finalized late in the campaign, but were used for the evaluation.

In crowdsourcing annotation, such mini-references are quite common, and are used to validate the work of the participants. For example, in Phrase Detectives [CHA 08] and ZombiLingo [FOR 14b], a reference corpus annotated by experts of the task is used for the training and evaluation of the players.

It has to be noted that building a mini-reference represents a "mini-campaign" inside the campaign. Consequently, the steps described in sections 1.1.5 and 1.1.6 also apply to the mini-reference. However, in practice, the break-in period and the publication are not needed.

1.1.4.2. Training the annotators

The training of the annotators is now recognized as essential to the quality of the annotation (see, among others [DAN 09, BAY 11]) and should be taken into account in the annotation campaign.

Usually, the annotators are trained for the task, i.e. both on the annotation itself and on the tool used for it. However, the two trainings present different types of difficulties. For annotators who are very competent in their domain but not at ease with computers, it is important to find the most appropriate tool, even if it means being a little less efficient (for example, a point-and-click tool like Glozz). Note that getting familiar with the tool can take more time than expected for these annotators. The training phase can also be used to detect annotators who are unable to perform the task correctly and to exclude them.

The training is done on an extract from the mini-reference, which has to be annotated by the annotators using the annotation tool and according to the provided guidelines. If possible, a first collective training session, with all the annotators, is more profitable than distant training, as they can ask all the questions they want and get all the answers at once.

This first collective phase should be followed by another phase during which the annotators work in real conditions and in parallel, without consulting each other, on the same sub-corpus, tracking their time. This tracked time will be used to visualize the learning curve of the annotators, like we did with ours on the *Penn Treebank* (see Figure 1.3). This curve is the first indicator of the level of training of the annotators. The second indicator is the produced quality.

The evaluation of the training can be done on the mini-reference (accuracy or F-measure) or between annotators (inter-annotator agreement). A discussion should be organized with the annotators to explain the difficult points (the ones on which they disagree the most between themselves or with the reference).

The training phase can expose errors or imprecisions in the annotation guide and thus lead to modifications of the guidelines and of the mini-reference.

In games like `Phrase Detectives` or `ZombiLingo`, the training phase is automatized (indications are provided to the players to help them train themselves during the tutorial phase) and ends only when the player performs sufficiently well (less than 50% errors on `Phrase Detectives` for example).

On the contrary, in microworking platforms, the annotators can at best be submitted to a competency test before starting to work, but to our knowledge, no training phase is planned in the system.

We will see in the next chapter that training and crowdsourcing are not contradictory, but to associate them questions what some consider to be one of the fundamental principles of the system: the participation of "non-experts". Is training "non-experts" not the same as transforming them into experts, at least of the task?

1.1.5. *Annotation*

1.1.5.1. *Breaking-in*

The end of the pre-campaign does not immediately correspond to a definitive stabilization of the campaign. First, the training of the annotators will continue, since they rarely reach the maximum of their possibilities at the end of the pre-campaign (for the POS annotation of the *Penn Treebank*, the learning period lasted one month). Second, the annotation guide will be modified again, according to the annotators' remarks. Therefore, their annotations will possibly have to be corrected.

A more or less long break-in period thus succeeds to the pre-campaign. Depending on the available means, the manager will continue to modify the guide more or less late in the campaign. The ideal would be to be able to review it until the very end of the campaign, in order to take into account all the elements discovered in the corpus. In practice, the guide needs to be stabilized so that the annotators can progress in the annotation and do not spend too much time correcting what they have already annotated. A good moment for that is probably when they reach their cruising speed (it can be detected easily as can be seen in Figure 1.3).

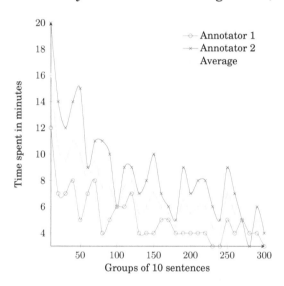

Figure 1.3. *Learning curve for the POS annotation of the* Penn Treebank *[FOR 10]. For a color version of the figure, see www.iste.co.uk/fort/nlp.zip*

This break-in phase also exists in crowdsourcing. The design of the game or of the microworking task requires several trials before the instructions (the minimal annotation guide), the interfaces (annotation tools) and the conditions of the annotation (for example with or without time limitation) are optimized. An example of these iterations is presented in [HON 11].

1.1.5.2. *Annotating*

The vast majority of the work will be carried out by the annotators during the annotation phase. The preceding steps allowed us to prepare it, but it is still important that the annotators be monitored by the expert or the manager on a regular basis.

Inter-annotator agreement metrics should be computed regularly, to check that the annotation is reliable (see Figure 1.4). This implies that at least partial parallelization is planned. Depending on the available time, the annotation can be performed totally in parallel, by at least two annotators, but most of the time only parts of it will be. In crowdsourcing, however, it is quite common to have the participants annotate all the corpus in parallel.

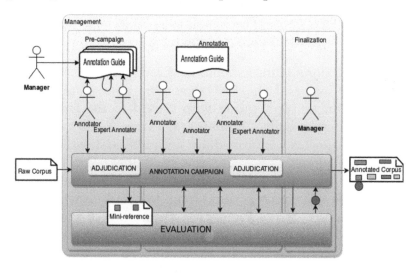

Figure 1.4. *The annotation process, revisited (simplified representation)*

The annotation phase itself can include an automatic pre-annotation step. In this case, the work of the annotators is limited to correcting this existing annotation and to complete it if necessary. We carried on a very systematic study on pre-annotation with Benoît Sagot in [FOR 10], which showed that, at least on English POS annotation, there is a bias due to the pre-annotation (attention slips from the annotators, who rely too much on the pre-annotation). However, the observed gains are such (twice the speed of annotation, even with a low accuracy tool) that it is worth warning the annotators of the dangers in the guidelines. The task itself is not fundamentally different, so we will use the term annotation in those cases too.

Each annotator in the campaign is assigned some files to annotate. They are provided with the up-to-date annotation guide, which is coherent with the used data model, and an appropriate annotation tool. They have been trained for the task and they have assimilated the principles explained in the guide. The break-in period should have helped them in refining their understanding of the task.

Ideally, the guidelines should be directly integrated in the annotation tool and the tool should be able to check the conformity of the annotation with regard to the guidelines, but if this was possible, human annotators would no longer be needed. However, intermediary features exist, which allow for a more efficient usage of the guidelines. The first one consists of providing an easy access to the guidelines, using for example a hypertext link from the tool. Another one would be to have the tool apply constraints which are defined in the guidelines (this was done with `EasyRef` in the EASy campaign, see Appendix A.2.2). The minimum is to ensure that the guidelines and the data model used in the tool are consistent (`Slate` includes for example a general versioning of the annotation, see Appendix A.4.1).

The annotation tool used by the annotators should help them not only in annotating, but also in monitoring their progression on the files which were assigned to them, in tracking the time spent on each file (or on each annotation level) and in notifying the expert or the manager of problems. It should also provide some advanced searching features (in the categories and in the text), so that the annotators can efficiently correct their annotations.

During the annotation phase, a regular evaluation of the conformity of the annotation with regards to the mini-reference should be done, associated with regular intra- and inter-annotator agreement measurements.

1.1.5.3. *Updating*

Even if it has been decided to stabilize the guidelines at the end of the break-in phase, updates are inevitable during the pre-campaign and the break-in phase. These updates have to be passed on to the annotated corpus, in order for it to remain consistent with the guidelines.

During the pre-campaign, updates are decided informally, between experts. The mini-reference being small by definition, the corrections can be made immediately.

During the break-in period, updates are either formally decided upon by the manager, following disappointing evaluations or less formally by the annotators, who ask the expert(s) or the manager to modify the guidelines. The manager can decide to give up on some of them for reasons of cost.

1.1.6. *Finalization*

Once the corpus is annotated, the manager has to finalize the campaign. He/she has at his/her disposal the annotations added to the corpus and a series of indicators, including at least evaluation metrics (conformity and intra- and inter-annotator agreement results), and sometimes uncertainty features added by the annotators. The manager can run a quick questionnaire among the annotators to try and catch their impressions concerning the campaign. Then he/she has to decide what to do next. Four options are available:

1) publish the corpus, which is considered to be in a sufficiently satisfactory state to be final;

2) review the corpus and adapt the annotation guide;

3) adjudicate the corpus;

4) give up on revision and publication (failure).

In most cases, a correction phase is necessary. If the annotation was carried out totally in parallel by at least two annotators, this correction can correspond to an adjudication by an expert, but it is most of the time performed more or less automatically, using the indicators provided during the campaign.[7]

In case there is a correction (adjudication and reviewing), the corpus has to be evaluated and be submitted, with its indicators, to the decision of the manager, who can either publish the corpus or have it corrected again.

1.1.6.1. *Failure*

A complete failure, which would be noticed at the end of the campaign (during finalization) is a sign of an absence of management and remains rare. However, we witnessed such a case of failure in the campaign described in [FOR 09]. It was due to a series of causes, the main one being that there was no real manager in charge of the campaign.

1.1.6.2. *Adjudication*

The adjudication is the correction by one or more expert(s) of the annotations added by the annotators. This correction is usually limited to the disagreements between annotators

---

7 It has to be noted that corrections in the annotated corpus can also be done during the annotation phase itself. Therefore, it is important that the annotation tool provide a powerful search tool.

(hence the name), but we extend here its definition to the correction by an expert of all the annotations (a rare case in traditional annotation). In the first case, the expert validates (or not) one of the concurrent annotations. The annotations have therefore to be sorted prior to the adjudication, so that the expert only decides on disagreements. The expert can also be called for punctually, to decide on a case that is particularly difficult to annotate.

In all cases, the work of the expert can be facilitated using a tool, for example an adapted interface showing in parallel the conflicting annotations.

Interestingly, microworking à *la* Amazon Mechanical Turk does not exempt from manual correction. For example, in [KAI 08], PhD students were hired to validate the questions/answers corpus. In Phrase Detectives the corrections are made by the players themselves, who judge annotations added by others.

1.1.6.3. *Reviewing*

In most annotation campaigns, the available resources are not sufficient to manually correct the entire annotated corpus. The correction is therefore more or less automatized, from the indicators gathered during the annotation phase. When errors are consistent, they can be corrected globally on the whole corpus, without the need for an expert.

The manager (associated with an expert, if he/she is not one) can decide to merge two categories that are too ambiguous. The annotation then needs to be modified. He/she can also remove one or two categories if their annotation was problematic. Finally, he/she can decide not to take into account the annotations from a specific annotator, if they diverge too much (in particular in crowdsourcing).

Semi-automatic correction procedures were used in the structured named entity campaign in old press. These corrections were identified thanks to a manual analysis of the errors carried on on a sample of the annotated corpus.

1.1.6.4. *Publication*

It is essential that the quality of the reviewed annotated corpus (or final corpus) is evaluated. In the case of a correction through adjudication of the disagreements, an evaluation performed by an expert of a random sample of uncorrected elements can be sufficient to evaluate the quality of the final corpus. In the (rare) case of a total correction of the annotated corpus, such a final evaluation is not needed, but can be carried out by a different expert on a sample of the corpus.

This final evaluation can be used as a seal of approval of the annotated corpus and can be taken into account during the evaluation of systems trained with this corpus. The corpus is published with its up-to-date annotation guide, if possible with a version number.

In all cases, the indicators provided with the annotated corpus are crucial to the manager.

1.2. Annotation complexity

What is complex? What should we automatize? In which case? An important step in the preparation of an annotation campaign is to identify the complexity dimensions of the annotation task at hand, as it allows us to better plan the annotation work and to put the right tools at the right place. However, this is far from being trivial, as everything seems entangled like in a wood ball.

We worked on the subject with Adeline Nazarenko (LIPN/University of Paris 13) and Sophie Rosset (LIMSI-CNRS), using the various annotation projects in which we participated as a basis for our analysis. We identified and tested six complexity dimensions which we believe to be universal to all annotation tasks and we presented them in [FOR 12d]. We provide here what we hope to be a more pedagogical (and a slightly simplified) view on these complexity dimensions, trying to improve their presentation by taking into account the feedback we got on the main article.

The six complexity dimensions we will describe here are all independent of each other, except for one, the context. Identifying them for a specific annotation campaign means disentangling the wood ball. It may seem a little confusing at first, because we are not used to considering the complexity of a task as independent dimensions. However, this mental effort is essential to the deep understanding of an annotation task and we observed that the complexity grid we propose represents a very useful guide to changing perspectives on a campaign.

In order to be able to visualize the result globally without reforming another wood ball, we decided to associate metrics with each dimension, which, once computed, give results between 0 (null complexity) and 1 (maximum complexity). Some of these metrics can be computed *a priori* (without any annotation done yet) while others require an annotation sample or annotations from a similar campaign. Note that these metrics are independent from the volume to annotate and the number of annotators.

An example of visualization is shown in Figure 1.5 using a spiderweb diagram. The blue lines correspond to the dimensions linked to the identification of the segment to annotate, the three red lines to the dimensions related to the added note and the green one is the context. Instantiated examples will be given later on.

1.2.1. *Example overview*

First, let us have a look at examples of annotation in NLP. We take three, in which we participated either as annotators (the *Penn Treebank* part-of-speech annotation,[8] and the structured named entity annotation) or as campaign manager (the gene renaming campaign). We believe they correspond to a large enough variety of situations to illustrate the complexity dimensions presentation we are going to make.

Figure 1.5. *Visualization of the complexity dimensions of an annotation task. For a color version of the figure, see www.iste.co.uk/fort/nlp.zip*

1.2.1.1. *Example 1: POS*

In the *Penn Treebank* part-of-speech (POS) annotation campaign, the corpus was pre-annotated and the annotators had to correct the provided annotations. As can be seen on Figure 1.6, the annotations were added in-line (inserted in the text itself),[9] separated from the original text by a simple marker (a slash), in a simple text editor. Like in any POS annotation campaign, all the lexical units[10] were annotated.

I/PRP do/VBP n't/RB feel/VB very/RB ferocious/JJ ./.

Figure 1.6. *POS annotation in the Penn Treebank [MAR 93]. For a color version of the figure, see www.iste.co.uk/fort/nlp.zip*

---

8 Obviously we did not participate in the original campaign, but we re-annotated part of the corpus for the experiments we led for [FOR 10].

9 We put them in blue here for easier reading.

10 In the *Penn Treebank*, these were tokens.

1.2.1.2. *Example 2: gene renaming*

Gene renaming annotation, on the other hand, implied annotating very few segments in the whole corpus (in average one renaming per file). The annotators had to identify the gene names involved in a renaming relation and annotate the former name of the gene and its new name (see Figure 1.7). Due to constraints imposed by the annotation tool, Cadixe [ALP 04], which was already in use when we joined the project, the annotators could not annotate the relation as such. The annotations in XML therefore included an identifier (<Former id="1">, <New id="1">), were added in-line and rendered in corresponding colors (one per renaming relation) by the tool. The corpus was not pre-annotated.[11]

> The yppB:cat and ypbC:cat null alleles rendered cells sensitive to DNA-damaging agents, impaired plasmid transformation (25- and 100-fold), and moderately affected chromosomal transformation when present in an otherwise Rec+ B. subtilis strain. The yppB gene complemented the defect of the recG40 strain. yppB and ypbC and their respective null alleles were termed recU and "recU1" (recU:cat) and recS and "recS1" (recS:cat), respectively. The recU and recS mutations were introduced into rec-deficient strains representative of the alpha (recF), beta (addA5 addB72), gamma (recH342), and epsilon (recG40) epistatic groups.

Figure 1.7. *Gene renaming annotation [JOU 11]. For a color version of the figure, see www.iste.co.uk/fort/nlp.zip*

1.2.1.3. *Example 3: structured named entities*

Finally, in the structured named entity annotation campaign, the work was done from scratch (no pre-annotation) on an advanced text editor (XEmacs), with a specific plug-in allowing the annotators to select the

---

11 We made some tests and pre-annotation did not really help as most gene names were not in a renaming relation, thus generating a lot of noise, and some could not be found by our pre-annotation tool (silence).

appropriate tags step by step following the structure of the tagset. For example, if the annotator selected the segment "Lionel" and the tag *pers*, the tool then proposed the subtypes *ind* or *coll* (for a theoretical illustration of the annotation, see Figure 1.8). Obviously, not all the text was annotated; however, it represented a much larger proportion than in the case of gene renaming. It should be noted here that the corpus was in French and some of it was transcribed speech (broadcast news) [ROS 12].

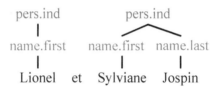

Figure 1.8. *Structured named entity annotation [GRO 11]*

These three annotation campaigns are so different that it seems difficult to compare them in terms of complexity. We will see that the complexity dimensions allow for that too.

1.2.2. *What to annotate?*

The first logical step in the manual annotation is to identify the segment of the signal to annotate. This "identification" consists, in fact, of two movements: (i) extracting, in a rather gross way, a piece to annotate from the signal (discrimination) and (ii) delimiting the precise boundaries of this segment.

1.2.2.1. *Discrimination*

If the second step is easy to grasp for most people, as delimitation builds on existing metrics like the word error rate (a well-known metric of the performance of speech recognition systems), the first step, the discrimination phase, is usually more difficult to understand and is often overlooked. This dimension is important, as it captures the "needle in a haystack" effect, i.e. the fact that the segment to annotate is more or less easy to find in the source signal.

Let us consider examples 1 and 2. In POS annotation (example 1), all the tokens need to be annotated; there is nothing to search for (especially as the corpus was pre-annotated), so the discrimination will be null (0). On the contrary, in the gene renaming annotation case (example 2), the segments to annotate are scattered in the corpus and rare (one renaming per text on average), so the discrimination will be very high (close to 1).

When the segments to annotate are lost in the crowd of the text, i.e. when the proportion of what is to be annotated as compared to what could be annotated (resulting from the default segmentation, often token by token) is low, the complexity due to the discrimination effort is high. This is expressed in the following way:

DEFINITION 1.1.–

$$Discrimination_a(F) = 1 - \frac{|A_a(F)|}{|D_i(F)|}$$

where F is the flow of data to annotate, a is an annotation task, $|D_i(F)|$ is the number of units obtained during the segmentation of F at level i and $|A_a(F)|$ is the number of units to be annotated in the relevant annotation task.

Applying this metric, we obtain a discrimination of 0 for POS annotation and 0.95 for gene renaming.

1.2.2.2. Delimitation

Once the units are roughly identified, they have to be finely delimited. This is the delimitation process.

The definition of the delimitation metric is inspired by the slot error rate (an adaptation of the word error rate) [MAK 99]:

DEFINITION 1.2.–

$$Delimitation_a(F) = min(\frac{S + I + D}{|A_a(F)|}, 1)$$

where $|A_a(F)|$ is the final number of discriminated units, I is the number of inserted units, obtained by initial unit decomposition, D is the number of units deleted when grouping some of the initial units and S is the number of substitutions, i.e. the number of discriminated units that underwent a change in their boundaries other than that of the previous decomposition and grouping cases.

The delimitation complexity dimension is null in the case of gene renaming, as gene names are simple tokens. It reaches the maximum (1) for the structured named entity task, as many frontier changes have to be performed by the annotators from a basic segmentation in tokens.

The computation of both the discrimination and the delimitation complexity dimensions requires at least a sample of annotation, either from the campaign being prepared or from a previous, similar campaign.

1.2.3. *How to annotate?*

Once precisely identified, the units have to be characterized by the annotators. To do so, they rely on an annotation language with a certain expressiveness, instantiated in a tagset of a certain dimension.

1.2.3.1. *Expressiveness of the annotation language*

To evaluate the complexity due to the expressiveness of the annotation language, we decided to rely on an arbitrary (but logical) scale, graduated from 0.25 (type language) to 1 (higher order languages). Relational languages of arity 2 are attributed 0.5 in complexity and 0.75 is associated with relational languages with arity higher than 2.

In the simplest and most frequent case, the annotation language is a type language: annotating consists of associating a type with a segment of data. A lot of annotation tasks use this category of language: POS, speech turns, named entities, etc. The number of tags can vary, but this does not change the expressiveness of the language.

Establishing relations between units has become a relatively common task, but it is more complex. It requires us to connect different segments of data, which are often typed. The relations are often typed too and they can be oriented. This is for example the case for dependency syntax relations or gene remaining annotation.

In general, the relations are binary, but sometimes relations of arity above two are necessary, for example in information extraction: who bought what? when? to whom? at which price? In such cases, the annotation task is much more complex: the annotators have to discriminate, delimit and categorize the arguments of the relation, then to identify the couples, triplets, n-uplets of segments to annotate and finally, to label the relation.

Higher order languages are used when annotations are added to annotations, for example to qualify an annotation as uncertain. However, the complexity of this type of language is such that, in most cases, the problem is avoided by increasing the dimension of the tagset (creating a new feature associated with the main types).

Most annotation tasks correspond to a complexity of 0.25 or 0.5 for this dimension. In our examples, the POS and structured named entity annotation tasks are performed using simple type languages, so they reach a complexity of 0.25. Interestingly, the gene renaming campaign, that should correspond to 0.5 as it is a relation, reaches only 0.25 in complexity, due to the fact that the annotation tool did not allow for the annotation of real relations. Although it simplified this complexity dimension, it made the tagset more complex to use.

1.2.3.2. *Tagset dimension*

The size of the tagset is probably the most obvious complexity dimension. It relates to short-term memory limitations and is quite obvious when you annotate. However, a very large number of tags is not necessarily a synonym for maximum complexity: if they are well-structured, like in the structured named entity annotation task (31 types and sub-types), then the annotators have to make choices from a reasonable number of tags each time, at different levels. In the structured named entity case (see Figure 1.9) they first have to choose between seven main types (*Person, Function, Location, Production, Organization, Time, Amount*), which corresponds to a degree of freedom of 6. Then, in the worst case (if they selected *Production*), they have to choose between nine sub-types, i.e. a degree of freedom of 8. Finally, sub-subtypes are available in some cases like *Location* and *Time*, so there can be a choice to make from a maximum of four tags, which corresponds to a degree of freedom of 3. We propose to use these degrees of freedom to compute the tagset dimension complexity, in order to take into account the fact that tagset constraints relieve the annotators from part of the categorizing effort.

The total degree of freedom ν for the choice of m labels is given by the following formula:

$$\nu \leq \nu_1 + \nu_2 + \ldots + \nu_m$$

where ν_i is the maximal degree of freedom the annotator has when choosing the ith tag ($\nu_i = n_i - 1$).

The tagset dimension can then be computed using the following formula:

$$Dimension_a(F) = min(\frac{\nu}{\tau}, 1)$$

where ν is the global degree of freedom the annotator has when choosing a tag for an annotation task a within a flow of data F, and τ is the threshold from which we consider the tagset as arbitrarily large. In the experiments detailed below, τ is worth 50, based on the feedback of the annotators, but it can be adapted if necessary.

Person			Function		
pers.ind (individual person)	*pers.coll* (group of persons)		*func.ind* (individual function)	*func.coll* (collectivity of functions)	
Location			Production		
administrative (*loc.adm.town, loc.adm.reg, loc.adm.nat, loc.adm.sup*)	physical (*loc.phys.geo, loc.phys.hydro, loc.phys.astro*)	facilities (*loc.fac*), oronyms (*loc.oro*), address (*loc.add.phys, loc.add.elec*)	*prod.object* (manufactured object)	*prod.serv* (transportation route)	*prod.fin* (financial products)
			prod.doctr (doctrine)	*prod.rule* (law)	*prod.soft* (software)
			prod.art	*prod.media*	*prod.award*
Organization			Time		
org.adm (administration)	*org.ent* (services)		*time.date.abs* (absolute date), *time.date.rel* (relative date)	*time.hour.abs* (absolute hour), *time.hour.rel* (relative hour)	
Amount					
amount (with unit or general object), including duration					

Figure 1.9. *The tagset dimension: taking the structure into account in the structured named entity annotation task [GRO 11]*

Using these formulas, the tagset dimension complexity of the structured named entity annotation task reaches 0.34, which is quite low as compared to the 0.62 we would obtain without taking the structure into account.[12] As for the gene renaming annotation task, it involved only two tags, *Former* and *New*, but to bypass the annotation tool constraints, an identifier had to be added to disambiguate between the renaming couples that were present in the same text. As there were no more than ten renaming relations per text, this represents around 10 "subtypes", i.e. ν is close to 10 and the tagset dimension reaches 0.2, which is not so far from the result for structured named entities.

---

12 These results differ from the ones presented in [FOR 12d] because we simplified the example (the annotation task also included components).

Both the expressiveness of the language and the tagset dimension can be computed *a priori*, without any annotation done yet, provided the tagset has been defined.

1.2.3.3. *Degree of ambiguity*

Disambiguating the units to annotate is at the heart of the work of the annotators. This is obviously a complexity dimension and this is where most of the interpretation lies, but it is very difficult to evaluate precisely. However, we propose two ways of approximating it.

1.2.3.3.1. Residual ambiguity

First, we can observe the traces left by the annotators when they are given the opportunity and the possibility to do so. For example, in a gene and protein names annotation campaign [FOR 09], we gave the annotators the possibility to add an uncertainty feature to the annotation (see Figure 1.10). Although one of them used this possibility, it is quite useful to evaluate the ambiguities they faced.

> [...]   <EukVirus>3CDproM<   /EukVirus> can process both structural and nonstructural precursors of the <EukVirus **uncertainty-type** = "too-generic"><taxon>poliovirus<   /taxon> polyprotein< /EukVirus> [...].

Figure 1.10. *Example of typed trace left by the annotator when annotating gene and protein names [FOR 09]*

We call this the *residual ambiguity* and we define it in a very simple way:

DEFINITION 1.3.–

$$Ambiguity_{Res,a}(F) = \frac{|Annot_A|}{|Annot|}$$

where a and F are the annotation task and the flow of data to be considered and where $|Annot_A|$ and $|Annot|$ are respectively the number of annotations bearing an ambiguity mark and the total number of annotations added to F.

By definition, the residual ambiguity can only be computed from an annotation sample, if the possibility to add traces was given to the annotators. In the gene renaming campaign, it was nearly null (0.02), probably due to the fact that, again, only one annotator added traces. This metric is not completely reliable and it should be associated with another one whenever possible.

1.2.3.3.2. Theoretical ambiguity

The second way to measure the complexity of the disambiguation process is to measure the degree of *theoretical ambiguity* for the tasks where several occurrences of the same vocable are annotated. This applies to POS annotation or semantic disambiguation, but not to gene renaming annotation.

This metric relies on the idea that ambiguous vocables are annotated with different tags in different places in the text (or flow of data). We then need to compute the proportion of the units to annotate which correspond to ambiguous vocables, taking into account their frequency. This can be done using the following formula:

DEFINITION 1.4.–

$$Ambiguity_{Th,a}(F) = \frac{\sum_{i=1}^{|Voc(F)|} (Ambig_a(i) * freq(i, F))}{|Units_a(F)|}$$

with

$$Ambig_a(i) = \begin{cases} 1 \text{ if } & |Labels_a(i)| > 1 \\ 0 \text{ else} \end{cases}$$

where Voc is the vocabulary of the units of the flow of data F, $|Voc(F)|$ the size of the vocabulary, $freq(i, F)$ the frequency of the vocable i in F, $|Units_a(F)|$ the number of units to annotate in F and $|Labels_a(i)|$ the number of tags available for the vocable i for the annotation task a.

Again, to compute this metric, we need an annotation sample or results from a similar task.

1.2.4. *The weight of the context*

The context to take into account during annotation is an obvious complexity factor. However, this dimension is not independent of all the above-mentioned dimensions. It directly influences the discrimination, delimitation and disambiguation processes, as the larger the context, the more difficult it gets to identify the units to annotate and to disambiguate them. Nonetheless, we decided not to include it as a modifying factor of these three dimensions, first to keep them simpler, and second because of its strong identity.

In NLP, the context is traditionally the co-text taken into account by the systems. Despite some evolution (particularly in discourse annotation or semantic annotation like football), the sentence is still the favored processing unit in our domain. However, for the annotators, the context is not only the text they have to read to be able to annotate (identify and characterize) properly, but also the knowledge sources they need to consult. These sources usually include the annotation guidelines, but they may also be external sources, either identified during the campaign preparation, like nomenclatures *à la* SwissProt,[13] or be found by the annotators themselves, on the Web or elsewhere.

---

13 See: http://www.uniprot.org/.

Obviously, the more accessible and predictable the source, the less complex it is for the annotators to get the piece of information they need. As for the co-text, the larger the context to take into account, the more complex it is to annotate (see Figure 1.11).

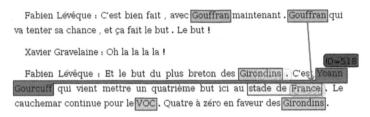

Figure 1.11. *Example of annotation of a goal in football annotation [FOR 12b]: a context of more than the sentence is needed*

We therefore designed a common discreet scale including both these sub-dimensions. In this scale, 0 corresponds to an impossible case, where there is no need for an annotation guide and no co-text to take into account. This should never happen, as the consensus has to be somehow transmitted to the annotators. 0.25 corresponds to a case where an annotation guide is needed OR the immediate co-text is needed to annotate. Logically, the complexity reaches 0.5 when the OR of the previous description changes to an AND, i.e. when the annotators need guidelines AND a small context to annotate. Another case in which we reach 0.5 is when a larger part of the data (like the sentence) OR an identified external source of knowledge is needed. 0.75 corresponds to the case when the annotators need to read a larger co-text AND have to consult an identified external source. It also covers the cases in which the annotators have to access unpredicted sources of knowledge OR have to read the whole text to be able to annotate. Finally, 1 is for cases where the annotators both have to consult previously unidentified sources of knowledge AND the whole data flow (usually, text).

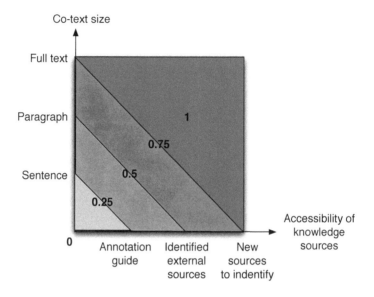

Figure 1.12. *The context as a complexity dimension: two sub-dimensions to take into account*

The gene renaming task is very complex from that point of view (1), as it required the annotators to read the whole text and they sometimes needed to consult new external sources. POS annotation would be close to 0.5, as most of the time only the guidelines and a small co-text are needed to annotate.

1.2.5. *Visualization*

Once the 6 complexity dimensions are computed, it is rather easy to put them into a spiderweb diagram to visualize the complexity profile of the annotation task. This type of representation can prove useful to compare the complexity of different tasks. Figures 1.13 and 1.14 present examples of what can be obtained applying the complexity grid, even in a fuzzy way (for the POS annotation task).

In the *Penn Treebank* POS annotation task, the corpus was pre-segmented and pre-annotated, so the discrimination and delimitation are null. The annotation language is a type language. The tagset contains 36 tags [SAN 90], so ν equals 35, but if we consider that there is an implicit structure in the tagset, with *JJR* and *JJS* being subtypes of *JJ*, then $\nu = 20 + 5 = 25$ and the complexity dimension of the tagset is 0.5. The annotation guidelines allowed for the usage of an ambiguity mark (a vertical slash, "|") in case of true ambiguities, so even if this is not exactly residual ambiguity, it can still be computed. However, for the *Wall Street Journal* part of the corpus, it represents only one case, so it probably can be considered as null over the whole corpus. As for the theoretical ambiguity, Dan Jurafsky and James H. Martin, in the new edition of their well-known book [JUR 09] evaluate the ambiguity in POS for English saying that "[...] the ambiguous words, although accounting for only 14–15% of the vocabulary, are some of the most common words of English, and hence 55–67% of word tokens in running text are ambiguous".[14] This implies that the theoretical ambiguity is rather high and without even computing it precisely, we can evaluate it at 0.5. The context to take into account is restricted to an annotation guide and a limited co-text (0.5).

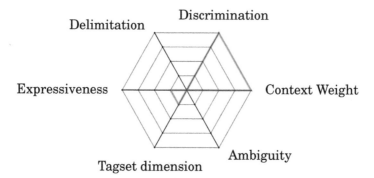

Figure 1.13. *Instantiated visualization: the delimited surface represents the complexity profile of the annotation task, here, gene renaming*

14 See the draft here: https://web.stanford.edu/jurafsky/slp3/9.pdf.

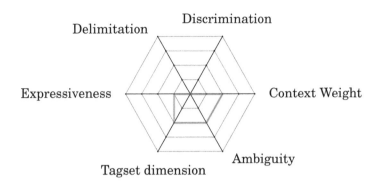

Figure 1.14. *Instantiated visualization: POS annotation in the Penn Treebank*

The complexity profiles of these annotation tasks are very different, thus reflecting the need for very different solutions to limit the complexity of the tasks. For POS annotation, even without pre-annotation, the discrimination and delimitation would have been low, due to the fact that, in this campaign, only tokens were annotated. However, the tagset dimension complexity could have been reduced by structuring the tagset more (and taking this structure into account in the annotation tool). As for the gene renaming campaign, it could have benefited from an "intelligent" pre-annotation (taking into account keywords like "renamed") to reduce the discrimination effort. It could also have been easier from the context point of view if a precise list of the sources to consult were provided in the guidelines.

1.2.6. *Elementary annotation tasks*

We saw that the gene renaming annotation task can be analyzed with the complexity grid as it was performed in the campaign, with identifiers as features in the XML tags. However, it should probably have been annotated differently, with a more suitable tool and with real relations. In this case, it would have been difficult to analyze it as a whole.

We propose to decompose such tasks into *Elementary Annotation Tasks* (EATs) and to compute the complexity of the various EATs independently, the global complexity of the task being a combination of the local EATs' complexity. Note that EATs do not necessarily correspond to annotation levels or layers [GOE 10] or to the practical organization of the work.

DEFINITION 1.5.– *An Elementary Annotation Task (EAT) is a task that cannot be decomposed. We consider that an annotation task can be decomposed into at least two EATs if its tagset can be decomposed into independent reduced tagsets. Tagsets are independent when their tags are globally compatible (even if some combinations are not allowed), whereas the tags from a unique tagset are mutually exclusive (apart from the need to encode ambiguity).*

In the gene renaming campaign, for example, the annotation of the relations can be analyzed as a combination of two EATs: (i) identifying gene names in the source signal and (ii) indicating which of these gene names participate in a renaming relation. The two tagsets are independent and the global task is easier to analyze in the following way.

1.2.6.1. *Identifying gene names*

Only a few words are gene names, so the discrimination is high (0.9). Gene names, in our case, are only tokens, so delimitation is null. The tagset dimension is null too, as there is only one tag (*gene name*). We use a type language (expressiveness=0.25). The ambiguity is very low, as only few gene names are ambiguous and the annotators left little trace of uncertainty on this. On the contrary, the necessary context is relatively high (between 0.5 and 0.75), as although only a few words are needed to identify a gene name, the annotators sometimes had to consult external sources.

1.2.6.2. *Annotating gene renaming relations*

This EAT consists of identifying, among all the gene name couples appearing in the same text (*PubMed* abstracts), the ones that are connected by a renaming relation, i.e. the ones that are the former and the new names of one gene. As we already said, renaming relations are rare, so the discrimination for this EAT is high (0.95). Gene names are already annotated (EAT 1), so delimitation is null. The relation is oriented, but there is only one type of relation, so the tagset is close to null. The annotation language is relational (0.5) and ambiguity is very low according to the traces left by the annotators (0.02). The context is maximum (1), as the annotators had to read the whole text to be able to identify renaming relations and they at least had to consult identified external sources.

The two EATs are then combined to provide a global view on the campaign with a scale that is twice the scale for one EAT (see Figure 1.15). In this particular case the result is very close to that of the single EAT analysis (compare with Figure 1.13).

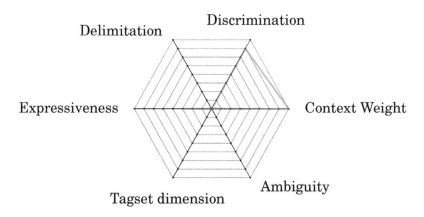

Figure 1.15. *Synthesis of the complexity of the gene names renaming campaign (new scale x2)*

Note that the decomposition into EATs does not imply a simplification of the original task, as is often the case for Human Intelligence Tasks (HITs) performed by *Turkers* (workers) on `Amazon Mechanical Turk` (see, for example, [COO 10a]).

1.3. Annotation tools

Once the complexity profile is established, the manager has a precise vision of the campaign and can select an appropriate annotation tool.

Annotation tools make manual annotation much easier, in particular when using markup languages like XML. These interfaces allow us to avoid the tedious writing of tags and the associated typing errors, but their contribution reaches far beyond that.

If there are many articles detailing a specific annotation tool, only a few provide a high level view on the subject. To our knowledge, only [DIP 04, REI 05] and [BUR 12] present an in-depth comparison of the tools in order to allow for their evaluation. However, these articles only consider a limited number of annotation tools (five in [DIP 04], two in [REI 05] and three in [BUR 12]) and the analysis carried out in the first two is focused on a specific annotation task (purely linguistic annotation in the first one and video annotation for the second one). The present state of the art uses some information from these articles, but it is mainly drawn from our own experience and analysis of the existing tools (a non-exhaustive list of these tools is presented in Appendix).

1.3.1. *To be or not to be an annotation tool*

Before going into more detail about annotation tools, we need to clarify what they are:

DEFINITION 1.6.– *A system supporting manual annotation, or annotation tool, is an interface facilitating the manual annotation of a signal.*

Some tools support the manual annotation of non-textual corpora, like video (Anvil[15] or Advene[16]), speech (Praat[17]) or music (wavesurfer[18]), but such an inventory would take us too far. We therefore restrain our analysis to manual text annotation.

We do not present Web annotation interfaces either, but their features are usually close to that of the tools we present here, without being as complex and rich. Finally, we do not consider XML or text editors as annotation tools as such. As this can seem surprising for some, we will explain why.

A number of manual annotation campaigns use XML editors to help the annotators in their work. This was the case for example for the manual annotation of Stendhal's manuscripts [LEB 08], which was performed using Morphon.[19] Another example is the *Definiens* project of annotation of the definitions of the French dictionary *Trésor de la Langue Française* [BAR 10], in which the annotators used oXygen.[20] Because we had to use XML tags, a partner imposed on us to use Epic[21] to annotate patents in pharmacology.

An XML editor is designed to edit XML files, not to annotate. If the features seem similar, the underlying logic is

---

15 See: http://www.anvil-software.de/.

16 See: http://liris.cnrs.fr/advene/.

17 See: http://www.fon.hum.uva.nl/praat/.

18 See: http://sourceforge.net/projects/wavesurfer/.

19 This tool is now deprecated, see: https://collab.itc.virginia.edu/wiki/toolbox/Morphon's.

20 See: https://www.oxygenxml.com/.

21 Now PTC Arbortext Editor: http://www.ptc.com/service-lifecycle-management/arbortext/editor.

quite different: an XML editor supports the modification of an XML file, not the annotation of a corpus of texts. The first difference concerns the notion of corpus, which does not exist in XML editors. This prevents us from having a global vision of the annotation. Moreover, these tools usually do not support standoff annotation, which prevents the easy annotation of overlaps, discontinuous groups and relations. Obviously, the management of annotation campaigns is not supported by such tools. Finally, some annotation tools (like Knowtator, Glozz, Slate or GATE) allow us to visualize the disagreements between annotators and for some of them to compute the inter-annotator agreement. This is never possible with an XML editor.

Text editors present the same limitations. In addition, they usually do not provide any means to validate the XML and annotators may therefore put the tags in the wrong order. However, simple tools can prove very useful for limited experiments (for example in prototyping) or when they are completed by normalization scripts.

Given the multiplication of annotation campaigns, it would take months to install and test all the annotation tools which are in use today. They are more or less available, more or less maintained, some are open-source, some not. From our point of view, the lifespan of a tool depends on the same criteria as that of corpora as described in [COH 05]: an annotation tool, to be used on the long-term, should be freely available, maintained and well-documented. This means that to survive on the long run, annotation tools like any software should be supported, either by a community of developers or by an institution. This kind of tool should also be easy to install and use. Ergonomics is important, as features which are difficult to access are not used by the annotators. We witnessed this in an annotation campaign in microbiology, in which the annotators often failed to report their uncertainties (which are needed to compute the residual ambiguity, see section 1.2.3.3) because the corresponding feature was not easy to add.

1.3.2. *Much more than prototypes*

Annotation tools are generally designed for one or several annotation tasks, rather than around the needs of the annotators. However, the tendency seems to evolve towards taking them more into account, through more user-friendly and more efficient interfaces. In addition, there is a growing consensus about the use of XML and standoff annotation, which seems to correspond to a form of standardization of the formalisms.

1.3.2.1. *Taking the annotators into account*

Even if there is still room for improvement (there are no keyboard shortcuts in Glozz [WID 09] and too many windows in MMAX2 [MÜL 06], etc.), the interfaces of the annotation tools are becoming more and more user-friendly. For example, they offer editing possibilities that allow the annotators to automate some tasks (*annotate all* in GATE [CUN 02], Glozz and Djangology [APO 10], automatically generated regular expressions in SYNC3 [PET 12], rapid selection with one selection in Knowtator [OGR 06]). They also often allow us to hide some annotations (by levels, or according to other criteria, like in Glozz) to ease the visualization and almost all of them allow for a certain level of customization (at least the colors of the tags).

Moreover, searching and editing annotations is sometimes made easier, thanks to powerful search engines, which allow us to search both the text and the annotations (in GlozzQL for Glozz, using regular expressions in UAM CorpusTool [O'D 08]). Once the annotators are trained for the task and with the annotation tool, they annotate more rapidly and more comfortably [DAN 09].

It has to be noticed that, even if it is not an equally shared preoccupation for all the annotation tools developers, the vast majority of the available interfaces are written in Java and therefore support most natural languages.

Some features, even if they are not yet widespread, are quite useful. For example, `brat` [STE 11] associates with each annotation a unique URL, which allows us not only to link the data over the Web, but also to unambiguously reference an annotation in the documentation. `Glozz`, which was designed for discourse annotation, offers a global visualization of the text that helps annotating macro level structures.

However, some useful features are still missing. For example, in a campaign where old press was annotated with named entities [ROS 12], we noted that the digitalized text was often erroneous and that the annotators needed to see the original image to be able to annotate correctly. For such cases, it would be interesting to include the original scanned source as an image into the tool. Another issue is that of meta annotations. If some tools like `Glozz` allow us to add commentaries or uncertainties, these have to be planned beforehand in the data model and are not proposed by default, even though they are essential.

Finally, most annotation tools are not robust enough and are not suitable for the annotation of large files (this is in particular the case for `Glozz` and `GATE`).

1.3.2.2. *Standardizing the formalisms*

XML has become the most widely used export and storage format for annotations, associated with standoff annotation in most tools. Annotations are standoff when they are presented separately from the source signal, often in another file. This evolution was advocated in [LEE 97, IDE 06]. Standoff annotation presents many advantages: it preserves the source corpus (the rights on this corpus are respected and it cannot be polluted) and it allows us to annotate discontinuous groups, overlaps, inclusions and relations (oriented or not). It is also more flexible than inline annotation since new annotation levels can be added, without modifying the existing ones. Finally, each annotation level can be manipulated separately, including in different files, in particular to compare annotations.

However, some annotation campaign managers prefer to give the annotators the possibility to access the source data. This was in particular the case in the structured named entity campaign in which we participated in [ROS 12]. In this case, the disadvantage is that an annotator may introduce errors in the file, for example by inserting XML tags in the wrong order, thus transforming it into an invalid XML file. GATE is the only tool we know of that offers the possibility to modify the source data as an option, leaving to the manager the choice of whether or not to allow such modifications.

The possibility to annotate relations (oriented or not) or sets (in the case of anaphora) is becoming more and more commonly proposed. However, Callisto [DAY 04] and GATE offer limited capabilities and UAM CorpusTool, Cadixe [ALP 04] and Eulia [ART 04] do not support this.

Some tools allow for the definition and usage of different annotation layers (MMAX2, Glozz, UAM CorpusTool), corresponding to linguistic levels (POS, syntax, etc.) or to "groups", which are defined by the designer of the data model, like in Glozz. The flexibility of the definition of these groups allows for the grouping of semantically close elements, without them having any specific linguistic meaning (like *Player*, *Team*, *Referee* and *Coach* in football matches annotation [FOR 12b]). These groups can then be used to annotate (one group being annotated before the other), to customize the display (hiding or not a group) and for the inter-annotator agreement computation.

1.3.3. *Addressing the new annotation challenges*

We observe that annotation tools are progressively reaching maturity and are evolving in three main directions: genericity, collaboration and campaign management.

1.3.3.1. *Towards more flexible and more generic tools*

We have witnessed, in the last decade, an evolution from task-oriented annotation tools towards more generic and more flexible tools, often using plug-ins (this is the case for example in GATE) or a common Application Programming Interface (API) (like in the LDC tools [MAE 04]).

This genericity, when it results from an evolution of a task-oriented tool or of a tool with a different objective, often generates complexity issues and the final tool is often difficult to install and to parameterize. This is the case, in particular, for GATE and Callisto, whose underlying logics are not so easy to understand (GATE, for example, was not originally designed for manual annotation). This results in a long learning curve for the campaign manager. When they are designed to be generic manual annotation tools from the very start, they are usually easier to get into and to parameterize. This is the case, for example, for WebAnno (see Appendix, section A.4.4) and CCASH [FEL 10].

Moreover, the generalization of XML allows us to adapt more easily to *de facto* standards like TEI (Text Encoding Initiative, a format that is well-known in the humanities), and thus to share annotated data.

Finally, some annotation tools designed for biocuration, like brat, include linked data annotation capabilities, which allow us to normalize the annotations using a unique identifier and to share them. This feature is very powerful and the development of linked data will accelerate its generalization. For the moment, linguistic linked data are still limited, but the development of new formats like NIF (NLP Interchange Format) [HEL 13] will certainly help.

1.3.3.2. *Towards more collaborative annotation*

As we saw in section 1.1, annotating implies to reach a consensus on the definition and perimeter of the used categories. This consensus is at the heart of the annotation process and it cannot be built without collaborating. Annotation is therefore by essence collaborative. However, we hope that we show in this book that collaboration in annotation can take various forms.

Georgios Petasis uses the adjective *collaborative/distributed* in [PET 12] to distinguish between collaborative annotation tools as Web applications and his tool, which is not a thin client. By doing so, he is trying to unravel two terms that are often mixed up today. The term *collaborative annotation* is ambiguous and for some means crowdsourcing annotation, for others annotation by a community of experts, if not both (the call for paper for the Linguistic Annotation Workshop VI is a good example of that),[22] and for others, including Petasis, it means the participation in a common annotation project.

Collaboration in annotation is defined along two axes: its visibility to the annotators (do they know they are collaborating?) and the potential means used for its implementation, as collaboration can be direct or indirect. For example, the wiki-like annotation mode, in which each annotator sees what the others are doing and can modify their annotations, like in brat and as an option in SYNC3, is fully collaborative, as it is both direct and visible to the annotators.

On the contrary, the adjudication by an expert (of the field of the annotation) of annotations added by others is a form of

---

22 *"The special theme for LAW VI is Collaborative Annotation (both community-based and crowd-sourced)"*: http://faculty.washington.edu/fxia/LAWVI/cfp.html

indirect collaboration, since the expert benefits from the work previously done and is inspired by it. Beyond that, annotating in parallel parts of the corpus and using the resulting inter-annotator agreement to improve the annotation guidelines, which in turn will be used by the annotators, is another form of collaboration since the work carried out by some upstream influences the annotation to be performed by all. This type of indirect collaboration is rather invisible to the annotators, as they only see its negative manifestation (when they are told about it): their disagreements.

A more obvious form of collaboration is the possibility to interact with other annotators and to keep track of these interactions. If in EasyRef this interaction is indirect through bug reports [CLE 08], it is direct and clearly visible in AnT&CoW [LOR 06][23] as a forum. Another benefit of this type of interaction is that it fosters the motivation of the annotators. Unfortunately, it is not yet offered in existing annotation tools for NLP. We plan to add such a feature to the Game With A Purpose (GWAP) ZombiLingo [FOR 14c], so that the annotators can both socialize and correct themselves.

Collaboration has always been part of annotation. However, we have been witnessing, since the advent of the Web 2.0, the development of new forms of collaboration. We present in details, in the second part of this book, the various forms of crowdsourcing annotation, but we can summarize here the main forms of collaboration it implies. Games with a purpose like Phrase Detectives [CHA 08] or ZombiLingo usually provide for an indirect and visible collaboration (through the obtained scores and the leaderboards).[24] As for the microworking platforms like Amazon Mechanical Turk, they only allow for a very indirect collaboration

23 AnT&CoW is not an annotation tool for NLP, which is why it does not appear in the Appendix.
24 Some future features of ZombiLingo will allow for more direct collaboration.

through the agreement (or disagreement) among the workers, which is invisible to them (they have very little feedback on their work).

This evolution is accompanied by a raising awareness of the importance of the annotators' training and of the evaluation of the annotation. Both Phrase Detectives and ZombiLingo put emphasis on these two points, with mandatory training and regular evaluations of the performance of the annotators. One of the objectives of collaboration is to facilitate the training of the annotators thanks to co-evaluation.

1.3.3.3. *Towards the annotation campaign management*

To our knowledge, the first research paper to explicitly mention annotation campaign management is [KAP 10], which presents SLATE, a tool that offers features not only to support the annotation process, but also, and this is what makes it original, a more macro vision of the annotation process, including a clear definition of its actors (*administrator* and *annotators*, considered as completely distinct). Thanks to SLATE, the administrator can distribute and monitor the texts to annotate and therefore manage the corpus. The corpus itself is versioned throughout the project and each annotation is identified with the version number of the project, which also corresponds to that of the tagset at the time of the annotation. SLATE also includes comparing and merging features.

A more formal and explicit definition of the roles can be found in GATE Teamware [BON 10], which identifies three of them (*campaign manager*, *editor* or *curator* and *annotator*) and in WebAnno [CAS 14] (*users*, *curator* and *administrators*). Egas distinguishes only between *managers* and *curators*. As for the annotation management features, they are similar in Djangology and GATE Teamware and were to be developed in CCASH and Callisto (but it does not seem to be done yet).

The evolution towards annotation management is now obvious. However, it started long before 2010. Interfaces that allow us to compare annotations and to compute inter-annotator agreements were added in many tools (Knowtator, MMAX2, Glozz, SYNC3). Besides, if NLP platforms like GATE propose automatic processing to optimize manual annotation, most of the other tools support the condition that such processing be applied beforehand (provided the result is adapted to the format of the tool, like in Glozz) and some even provide some pre-annotation, like *tag dictionary* (a unit is pre-annotated with the tags that are associated with it earlier in the corpus), in Djangology and CCASH.

Given the potential biases generated by pre-annotation [FOR 10], we consider that automatic processing should be decided upon and applied by the campaign manager. It therefore falls under campaign management and not annotation as such. The same goes for the possibility to modify the annotation schema during the campaign (this is proposed in UAM CorpusTool, GATE and ANALEC [LAN 12]).

Finally, tools like Slate or EasyRef[25] propose to define constraints on the annotation (for example, in EasyRef, pop up menus allowing only for the actions authorized in this context), which, again, should be defined by the manager.

The monitoring of the annotation campaign is another feature offered by many "simple" annotation tools that is directly linked to campaign management, even if it can be useful to annotators too. For example, brat can be configured to monitor the time spent by an annotator on a document and on each editing and typing action (a similar feature is proposed in CCASH). EasyRef keeps track of the activities on the system using logs. This monitoring, which is done locally

---

25 This tool is mentioned here because it offered interesting original features, but it was used only in one annotation project.

in annotation tools, is enriched by a more global management in annotation management tools like WebAnno, SLATE or GATE Teamware, which allows us to visualize the progress of the campaign and of the annotators. However, this feature requires that the notion of a corpus is taken into account, which is not the case in all annotation tools (it is for example absent in the annotation part of Glozz).

This evolution towards annotation management goes hand in hand with the multiplication of Web-based tools (WebAnno, Slate, Egas, etc.). This presents many advantages, in particular it offers the possibility to work from distance, but it can also be troublesome, for example for under-resourced languages annotation, as the annotators may have a limited Internet access.

1.3.4. *The impossible dream tool*

The rising diversity in annotations (see section I.2.1) implies a variety of annotation tools. From text to video or speech, from the micro level (POS annotation) to the macro level (discourse), a unique, universal annotation tool, which would satisfy the needs and constraints (for example, the preservation of the original format) of each and everyone seems inconceivable.

In addition, many annotation campaign managers would rather develop a new tool, adapted to the constraints of their campaign and which can be as simple as an old school Emacs plugin, than try and adapt to an existing tool, which would be time-consuming, could bias the annotation due to intrinsic limitations, and might in the end be disappointing.

If some tools are more used than others, often because they are well-featured and maintained (this is for example the case for GATE and WebAnno, and to a lesser extend, for Glozz and brat), there is yet, as of today, no annotation tool winning unanimous support. Developing a generic, reliable and well-documented annotation tool is a long-term endeavor. For example, it took two persons six months only to conceive Glozz and the same time to develop it.[26]

In addition, if there are many annotation tools available today, only a few of them provide features that allow to manage an annotation campaign. To our knowledge there are only a couple of them: Slate, GATE Teamware, Djangology, WebAnno and Egas [CAM 14]. Moreover, two of them present important limitations: Djangology is not maintained anymore and Egas is solely provided as an online service, specializing in biocuration. Finally, none of them propose any feature to prepare the campaign (see section 1.1). They provide no means to anticipate the complexities of the annotation campaign (see section 1.2) and to select the appropriate automation or inter-annotator metric to apply (see section 1.4). The analysis of complexity also provides useful information to select the most appropriate inter-annotator agreement metric.

The analyses of the annotation process and complexity dimensions presented in this chapter are therefore useful complements to your favorite annotation tool when preparing an annotation campaign.

1.4. Evaluating the annotation quality

1.4.1. *What is annotation quality?*

To be considered as "good", an annotation has to be valid, i.e. the notes added to the source have to be of the correct type and associated with the right segment in the flow of data. However, manually annotating is by definition interpreting, therefore there is no such thing as a "(ground) truth". We cannot directly measure the validity of manual annotation, we can only measure its reliability, i.e. how

---

26 Yann Mathet, personal communication, January 12th, 2011.

consistent the annotators were in annotating. This reveals how well they assimilated the guidelines and how coherent these guidelines are.

This *reliability* can only be evaluated by computing the agreement between annotators, or inter-annotator agreement, which is obtained by comparing the annotations of the same text made by different annotators. In addition to the inter-annotator agreement, which allows us to measure the *stability* of the annotation, the agreement of the annotator with him or herself later in the campaign (the intra-annotator agreement) also needs to be computed, in order to capture the *reproducibility* of the annotation [GUT 04].

If computing the intra- and inter-annotator agreements is essential, it does not have to be done on the whole corpus, for obvious reasons of cost-effectiveness. However, we strongly advise to do this very early in the campaign, so as to identify and address the problems rapidly, as was done in [BON 05].

Finally, to complete the quality evaluation, it is essential to randomly check the annotations on which the annotators agree. In Składnica , a Polish treebank, 20% of the agreed annotations were in fact wrong [WOL 11].

The inter-annotator agreement research field has been very active in the past decade and is still evolving rapidly. We present here the main issues and metrics and refer the reader who would like to go further to more detailed articles, in particular [ART 08] and [MAT 15].

1.4.2. *Understanding the basics*

1.4.2.1. *How lucky can you get?*

The most obvious and simplest metric measuring the inter-annotator agreement is the *observed agreement* (A_o). It corresponds to the percentage of times the annotators agreed, i.e. the number of agreeing annotations times 100 over the whole number of annotations. This metric is very simple and easy to compute, but it should not be used as such as it does not take chance into account. Why is that important?

In order to demonstrate the influence of chance on the inter-annotator agreement results, let us take a very simple example.[27] In an annotation task involving two categories and no segmentation (like the two sides of a coin), two annotators who would pick any of the two categories randomly (like tossing the coin) would statistically agree half of the time ($A_o = 0.5$). Therefore, in this case, an observed agreement below this baseline would be very bad (worse than by chance). The main issue with this kind of metrics is that their real scale depends on the context of the campaign: the minimum that can be obtained by chance differs according to the number of categories and annotators. This makes the results very difficult to interpret.

But it can be worse. In the same case (two categories, A and B, and predefined segments) but with three annotators, it is impossible for them to completely disagree ($A_o \neq 0$): if Annotator 1 says A and Annotator 2 says B, Annotator 3 will necessarily agree with one of the first two annotators. So the observed agreement will at least be 0.33, even before taking chance into account (see Table 1.16).

Pairs	Annotations	Agreement
Annotators 1&2	A B	No
Annotators 1&3	A A	Yes
Annotators 2&3	B A	No

Figure 1.16. *Case of impossible disagreement, with 3 annotators and 2 categories*

27 This example was suggested to us by Yann Mathet, from GREYC-CNRS (personal communication, Fall 2015).

Now, let us make a detour and consider the "truth". If the right answer is A, then they succeed in 4 out of 6 times, so they are right 66% of the time. But if the right answer is B, then they succeed in 2 out of 6 times, so they are right 33% of the time. Finally, there can be a perfect inter-annotator agreement ($A_o = 1$), for example if the three annotators say A, and 0% truth (if the right answer was B). On the contrary, 100% success in finding the truth implies a perfect agreement.

The same campaign with only two annotators allows for a total disagreement. In one case (3 annotators) the scale begins at 0.33 and in the other (2 annotators), it starts at 0, without even taking chance into account.

1.4.2.2. *The kappa family*

As of today, the reference article on the subject of this family of inter-annotator agreement metrics is the one written by Ron Artstein and Massimo Poesio in 2008 [ART 08]. Its presents in details and very clearly these coefficients. We will focus here on the two most well-known, Scott's pi [SCO 55] and Cohen's kappa [COH 60]. These coefficients are applicable to two annotators only, but generalizations to more than two annotators are available, like Fleiss' kappa [FLE 71], a generalization of Scott's pi, or multi-κ, a generalization of Cohen's kappa [DAV 82].

Pi and kappa are computed from the observed agreement (A_o), but they take chance into account, which is represented in the *expected agreement* (A_e). Hence, the metrics are defined using the same formula:

$$\kappa, \pi = \frac{A_o - A_e}{1 - A_e}$$

The only element that differs is the way they evaluate chance, i.e. the expected agreement (A_e). In one case (pi), the categories are affected to units by chance mimicking the way they were actually affected by the annotators, but the annotators themselves are supposed to behave in the same way (their behaviors are averaged). In the other case (kappa), both the categories and the annotators can by chance behave according to the way they behaved in reality.

1.4.2.2.1. Scott's pi

This coefficient is also called K in [SIE 88] or Kappa in [CAR 96] (or Carletta's kappa). In pi, the distributions realized by chance by the annotators are equivalent, but the chance distribution of the units (u) between categories (k) is not homogeneous and it can be estimated by the *average* distribution generated during their annotation by the annotators. The expected agreement for pi (A_e^π) is therefore defined as follows, with n_k being the number of units annotated with k by the two annotators.

$$A_e^\pi = \sum_{k \in K} \left(\frac{n_k}{2u}\right)^2$$

1.4.2.2.2. Cohen's kappa

This coefficient models chance by hypothesizing that the distribution of units between categories can differ from one annotator to an other. In this case, the probability for a unit (u) to be affected by a category (k) is the product of the probability that each annotator assigns it in this category. The expected agreement (A_e^κ) is therefore defined as follows n_{c1k} being the number of assignments to k for annotator 1:

$$A_e^\kappa = \sum_{k \in K} \frac{n_{c1k}}{u} \cdot \frac{n_{c2k}}{u}$$

Note that, by definition, $\pi \leqslant \kappa$. Usually, κ and π give very close results [DIE 04], which means that there is little bias between the annotators. It is therefore useful to compute both coefficients to check that.

1.4.2.3. *The dark side of kappas*

The coefficients of the kappa family are very efficient, they take chance into account and are not so difficult to compute. For these reasons, they have been widely used in NLP. The problem is that they are not always appropriate. In particular, they require the number of markables (segments that could be annotated) for their computation. If it is obvious for certain tasks like POS annotation, in which all the tokens are markables, it is less easy to determine in tasks in which the discrimination is not straightforward, like in gene renaming annotation.

To illustrate this, we introduce here the most widely used representation of data for inter-annotator agreement, the contingency table. This type of representation allows us not only to immediately visualize the agreement between annotators (the diagonal of the table), but also to rapidly identify the specifics of a campaign, like the prevalence of a category, i.e. the fact that a category is used (much) more often than the others. For these reasons, we strongly advocate for the presentation of the contingency table of an annotation campaign in the accompanying articles, whenever possible (two annotators and not too many categories), like in [PAL 05]. We completely agree with what is said in [HRI 02]:

> "showing the two-by-two contingency table with its marginal totals is probably as informative as any measure".

We present in Table 1.1 a contingency table for a toy POS annotation task with 5 categories and 100 segments, imagined from the following *Penn Treebank* example:

I/PRP do/VBP n't/RB feel/VB very/RB ferocious/JJ./.

In POS annotation, all the segments get an annotation, so there is no "hole" in the pavement. In this case, $A_o = 0.87$, $A_e^\kappa = 0.2058$, $A_e^\pi = 0.2062$, $\kappa = 0.8363$ and $\pi = 0.8362$.

		Annot. 1					
		PRP	VBP	RB	JJ	Punct	Total
Annot. 2	PRP	15	0	0	0	0	15
	VBP	2	17	1	2	0	22
	RB	0	2	22	3	0	27
	JJ	0	1	2	13	0	16
	Punct	0	0	0	0	20	20
	Total	17	20	25	18	20	100

Table 1.1. *(Imaginary) contingency table for a toy example of POS annotation*

On the contrary, in the gene renaming campaign, very few elements from the source are annotated and the empty category (no annotation) corresponding to the markables, is overwhelmingly prevalent, with 18,878 tokens (see Table 1.2).

		Annot. 1			
		Former	New	No annotation	Total
Annot. 2	Former	71	13	23	107
	New	8	69	15	92
	No annotation	7	8	18,840	18,855
	Total	86	90	18,878	19,054

Table 1.2. *Contingency table for the gene renaming annotation campaign [FOR 12c]*

Considering all the tokens as markables, we obtain $\kappa \approx \pi = 0.98$.

Obviously, we could have chosen to consider the gene names as markables instead of the tokens (see Table 1.3). In this case, we obtain $\kappa \approx \pi = 0.77$.

		Annot. 1			
		Former	New	No annotation	Total gene names
Annot. 2	Former	71	13	23	107
	New	8	69	15	92
	No annotation	7	8	951	966
	Total gene names	86	90	989	1,165

Table 1.3. *Contingency table for the gene renaming annotation campaign with the gene names as markables*

We detailed in [GRO 11] experiments that we led in the structured named entity annotation campaign on the inter-annotator agreement results in which we showed that the results vary quite significantly depending on the way the markables are computed.

The conclusion we draw from these various experiments is that coefficients from the kappa family should be avoided in cases in which there are "holes in the pavement", i.e. when not all of the signal is annotated, as in such cases, the necessarily arbitrary decisions in the definition of the markables may generate a prevalence bias.

1.4.2.4. *The F-measure: proceed with caution*

In some annotation campaigns, metrics usually used for the evaluation of the performance of the systems, like the F-measure, are used to evaluate the produced manual annotation. Often, this type of metric is chosen just because it is provided by default in the annotation tool, like in GATE (which also provides Cohen's kappa and Scott's pi). Sometimes, this choice is made to avoid the problem of the definition of the markables for the computation of kappa, for example in the case of named entity annotation [ALE 10, GRO 11]. In fact, it was demonstrated in [HRI 05] that when the number of markables is very high, the coefficients from the kappa family tend towards the F-measure.

The F-measure was designed for information retrieval and is now widely used in NLP. It corresponds to the weighted average of recall and precision:

$$\text{F-measure} = 2.\frac{\text{precision}.\text{recall}}{\text{precision} + \text{recall}}$$

with recall and precision defined as follows:

$$\text{Recall} = \frac{\text{Nb of correct found annotations}}{\text{Nb of correct expected annotations}}$$

$$\text{Precision} = \frac{\text{Nb of correct found annotations}}{\text{Total nb of annotations}}$$

It is therefore easy to compute.

By definition, precision and recall require a reference annotation. In the case of manual annotation, we are (most of the time) building this reference, so it does not exist yet. However, one may consider that the work of one annotator can be used as a reference for the other(s). The F-measure is then computed for each category and the global metric is the average of the local ones. It does not have to be computed both ways, as the recall of one annotator is the precision of the other [HRI 05].

However, the F-measure does not take chance into account, and we observed that sometimes chance has a significant impact on the results. This limitation makes it less suitable for manual annotation evaluation than other, more specific, measures like γ.

1.4.3. *Beyond kappas*

A lot of metrics have been proposed or revived, especially in the past few years, most of them to overcome the default of the kappa family metrics. We present here only a couple of them, from the weighted coefficients family, in order to introduce the final one, γ, which is very promising.

1.4.3.1. *Weighted coefficients*

Weighted coefficients allow us to give more importance to some disagreements than to others. The coefficients we briefly present here are more detailed in [ART 08]: the weighted version of Cohen's kappa (κ_ω) [COH 68] and Krippendorff's Alpha (α) [KRI 04].

Both coefficients are based on the disagreement between annotators and use a distance between categories, allowing us to describe how distinct two categories are. The idea behind this is that all disagreements are not equal, that some should have more weight than others. For example, a disagreement between two main categories (*Noun* and *Verb*), is more important than a disagreement in sub-types (*VerbPres* and *VerbPast*).

κ_ω and α are defined as follows:

$$\kappa_\omega, \alpha = 1 - \frac{D_0}{D_e}$$

where D_0 is the observed disagreement between the annotators and D_e the expected disagreement, i.e. the chance disagreement. The expected disagreements in κ_ω and α are computed in a similar way as κ and π respectively and include the notion of distance between categories.

We will not detail the calculus of D_e, which is presented for both metrics in [ART 08]. These metrics suffer from a major bias: distances are defined manually, based on intuition or knowledge of the campaign, and do not depend on the reality of the annotation. Another limitation is that they are dedicated to categorization tasks and do not take what Krippendorff calls unitizing into account.

Krippendorff then proposed a series of coefficients to go beyond α: αU [KRI 04], which covers unitizing, $_u\alpha$ [KRI 13], which focuses on positioning and $_{c|u}\alpha$ [KRI 13], which deals with categories, but for now it has to be noted that $_u\alpha$ and $_{c|u}\alpha$ are not currently designed to cope with embedding or free overlapping between the units of the same annotator [MAT 15].

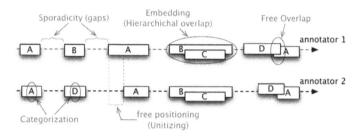

Figure 1.17. *Phenomena to take into account when computing inter-annotator agreements (Figure 1 from [MAT 15], by courtesy of the authors)*

1.4.3.2. γ: the (nearly) universal metrics

Yann Mathet and Antoine Widlöcher (GREYC-CNRS) designed the annotation tool `Glozz` and also created a new metric for the computation of the inter-annotator agreement, named γ,[28] which has been detailed in [MAT 15]. This metric is close to α in that it takes chance into account and does not require us to identify the markables. However, γ takes the nature of the units into account and, for example, two appended entities and a unique entity spanning two entities are considered differently in γ. The main advantage of γ is that it does not alter the annotations to compare them.

γ is holistic, in the sense that it takes the annotations from the whole corpus into account, rather than only local comparisons between units. It is also unified, as it does not dissociate between the alignment of the identified segments (discrimination and delimitation) and the agreement on the

---

28 An earlier version of this was called the "Glozz metrics" [MAT 11].

categories, both being performed simultaneously. Among the various possible alignments, γ keeps the one which minimizes the disagreement.

To do so, the metric relies on the notion of disorder of the system constituted by the set of annotations of a text. This disorder can be related to two types of dissimilarities, namely positional and categorial. The computation of the categorial dissimilarity requires, like in α and κ_ω, a distance between categories. This is the main weakness of the metric.

γ is defined as follows, for each annotation set j on a corpus c:

$$agreement(j) = \frac{e_{random}(c) - e(j)}{e_{random}(c)}$$

The entropy (the disorder) of an alignment of units corresponds to the average dissimilarities of its constituting units. The random entropy, $e_{random}(c)$, can be computed using different methods, including that presented in [MAT 11], which is implemented in Glozz. This method consists of observing the annotations produced by the annotators on the whole corpus and generating, independently of the text content, multi-annotations that respect the statistical distribution of the corpus, both in terms of positions and of categories.

The main issues with the metrics taking chance into account is that computing them is not always straightforward. It is especially the case for γ. The solution is to integrate the metric into an annotation tool, so that it can be computed directly using an interface. This is what has been done for γ, which is now rather easily computable in Glozz.

Interestingly, a technique is underused if it is not encapsulated in a tool, and if it is, it becomes a "black box" as defined by Bruno Latour [LAT 87], i.e. something that is no longer open, therefore no longer questioned. This is exactly what happened with GATE and the F-measure. However, it is quite different with Glozz and γ, as the tool and the metric were created first for manual annotation and the metric was well-tested before being integrated into Glozz.

For the moment γ is still little used, so it does not really allow for a comparison with older annotation campaigns. We therefore suggest to compute it as a complement to kappa, whenever possible.

Contrary to the annotation tools, we think that with γ the domain is now close to a rather universal solution, even if using a distance that is determined *a priori* is constitutes an important bias. In addition, the inter-annotator agreement for relations is still a major open issue, with no appropriate solution in sight.

1.4.4. *Giving meaning to the metrics*

Ron Artstein and Massimo Poesio detail in [ART 08] the different scales of interpretation of the Kappas that were proposed over the years (see Figure 1.18) and emphasize the fact that it is very difficult to define a meaningful threshold. What is a "good" agreement, as measured by kappa or another metric?

They conclude with caution, proposing a threshold of "reasonable quality" of 0.8 for the kappas, while adding that they "doubt that a single cutoff point is appropriate for all purposes". Other works, in particular [GWE 12] that presents various inter-annotator agreement metrics, insist on the problem of their interpretation. Another related issue is how to compare two different results obtained with different metrics.

Some studies concerning the evaluation of the quality of manual annotation allowed us to identify factors influencing the inter-annotator agreement, thus giving clues on the behavior of the metrics that were used. For example, it was demonstrated in [GUT 04] that the inter-annotator agreement and the complexity of the task are correlated (which is not surprising), in particular, the larger the tagset, the weaker the agreement. In the same article it is shown that there are only a limited number of categories generating disagreement. The meta study presented in [BAY 11] extends this research and identifies eight factors influencing the inter-annotator agreement: the "domain" (we would rather talk about the annotation type, as they compare word-sense disambiguation, prosodic transcriptions and phonetic transcriptions), the number of annotators, the training of the annotators, the annotation purpose, the knowledge of the domain, the language, the number of categories and the calculation method. The authors deduce from these recommendations to improve the quality of manual annotation. However, none of these analyses give a clear view on the behavior of agreement metrics or their meaning.

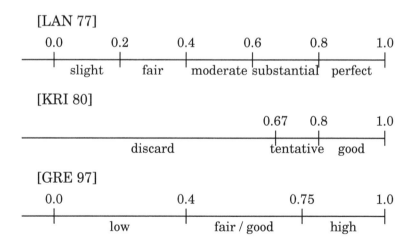

Figure 1.18. *Scales of interpretation of kappas (from the ESSLI 2009 course given by Gemma Boleda and Stefan Evert on inter-annotator agreement, by courtesy of the authors)*

We created a French working group on the subject, with people from LIMSI-CNRS (Sophie Rosset, Pierre Zweigenbaum, Cyril Grouin), LNE (Olivier Galibert and Juliette Kahn), INIST-CNRS (Claire François) and GREYC-CNRS (Yann Mathet and Antoine Widlöcher). Together, we discussed and reflected on the meaning of inter-annotator agreement metrics and the interpretation of the results. However, the original idea and the implementation of what is presented here come from Yann Mathet and Antoine Widlöcher. This work is detailed in [MAT 12]. We will present it here rapidly and complete it with real experiments led on the *TCOF-POS* corpus [BEN 12].

The idea proposed by Yann Mathet and Antoine Widlöcher is to reverse the problem and to analyze the results obtained with the various metrics on reference annotations (or artificial annotations), which are degraded in a controlled way.

1.4.4.1. *The Corpus Shuffling Tool*

This idea of applying controlled degradations to a reference is derived from research in thematic segmentation described in [PEV 02] and in [BES 09]. It was applied for the first time to inter-annotator agreement metrics in [MAT 11]. The principle is to generate degraded annotations in a statistically controlled way from a reference corpus. Several corpora are generated, corresponding to the different values of a deteriorated parameter, then the metrics are applied to the degraded corpora and their behavior can be observed.

The annotators produce errors that can be of various types and concern different dimensions. Each annotated unit can diverge from what it should be (a reference, imperfect by definition) in one or several ways:

– the delimitation of the unit is not correct (the frontiers do not correspond to the reference);

– the categorization of the unit is not correct (wrong category or wrong feature value);

– the discrimination of the unit is not correct: the annotation is not present in the reference (false positive);

– or, on the contrary, a unit from the reference is missing (false negative).

All these causes of errors in the annotation have to be taken into account in the inter-annotator agreement metrics. Mathet and Widlöcher developed a tool that generates "tremors" (i.e. degradations) along several dimensions.[29] These tremors are of various controlled magnitudes: the higher the magnitude, the more serious the errors. The obtained corpora with degraded annotations are then used to observe the behavior of the metrics according to different types of errors (dimensions) and a whole range of magnitudes. This allows us not only to compare the metrics (for a given magnitude, it is easy to compare the results obtained by the different metrics), but also to interpret the scores in a tangible manner (a given score for a given metric corresponds to a certain magnitude, of which we know the effects on the corpus). This tool takes as input the magnitude of error, from 0 (the perfect annotator) to 1 (the worst annotator, who annotates without even reading the text).

1.4.4.2. Experimental results

The experiments presented in [MAT 12] implied artificial annotations, i.e. annotations that were generated automatically from a statistical model describing the positional and categorical distribution of the markables. We will focus here on the obtained results rather than on the protocol, which is detailed in the article, and will present an experiment carried out on a real corpus.

---

29 This tool is freely available under a GPL license and will soon reappear here: http://www.glozz.org/corpusshufflingtool.

At the time of the experiments, the `Corpus Shuffling Tool` did not allow for a combination of paradigms to be taken into account. We therefore had to process segmentation and categorization separately. A first experiment was carried out on segmentation alone, rerunning the one described in [BES 09], comparing the generalized Hamming distance and WindowDiff, and adding γ. We will not present this experiment here, as it concerns metrics that cannot be considered as inter-annotator agreement metrics, since they require a reference. We simulated three annotators.

1.4.4.2.1. Artificial annotations

We present here results concerning the categorization process. The simulated situation is that of an annotation task in which the units to annotate are already localized, like in the *Penn Treebank* POS annotation. We created four annotation sets, including or not prevalence cases and a structured tagset, for which we consider that an error between a sub-category and a category should be considered as less serious than one between categories.

The `Corpus Shuffling Tool` was applied on these annotations to compare the following metrics: Cohen's kappa [COH 60], weighted kappa [COH 68], with two different weight matrices (the first one being much more lenient than the other) and γ, with or without the ability to deal with a structured tagset (taking the proximity between categories into account). An observed agreement (percentage of strict agreement between the three annotators) is also computed as baseline. The results of these experiments are shown in Figure 1.19.

These results show first that when there are no prevalence and no structured tagset (with different types of proximity between categories), all the compared metrics behave similarly (see Figure 1.19(d)), including the observed agreement (even if it slightly overestimates the agreement when the magnitude gets higher, because it does not take chance into account).

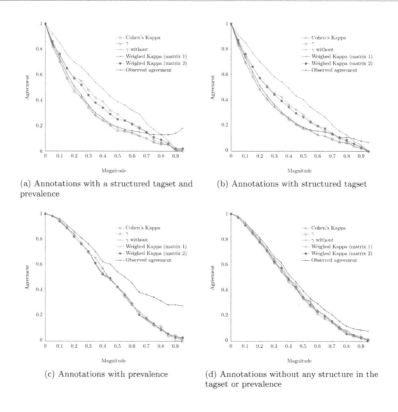

(a) Annotations with a structured tagset and prevalence

(b) Annotations with structured tagset

(c) Annotations with prevalence

(d) Annotations without any structure in the tagset or prevalence

Figure 1.19. *Comparison of the behaviors of the metrics on categorization. For a color version of the figure, see www.iste.co.uk/fort/nlp.zip*

In cases of prevalence of one category over the others (see Figure 1.19(c)), all the metrics continue to behave similarly, apart from the observed agreement, which tends to more and more overestimate the agreement, by nearly 0.25 at most. Chance has a significant impact here.

In case of a structured tagset, the weighted kappa and γ behave very differently than the other metrics. When taken into account, the more or less important proximity between categories, whether it is associated with prevalence or not (see Figures 1.19(a) and 1.19(b), respectively), generates noticeable differences, of 0.15 for γ and 0.25 for the weighted kappa. This can easily be explained by the fact that these metrics use a matrix actually describing the proximity between categories. Moreover, it is interesting to note that when applying these two metrics to data without a structured tagset (or at least without taking it into account), they behave almost exactly the same way as the simpler metrics which do not take the proximity into account (bottom figures). These metrics (γ and weighted kappa) are not biased, whatever the corpus.

As for the observed agreement, it is closer to the other metrics in cases where the tagset is structured, probably due to the fact that in cases of average magnitudes, proximity is more influential than prevalence. However, with a magnitude above 0.6, the observed agreement overestimates the agreement again.

1.4.4.2.2. Annotations from a real corpus

Since we were limited by the fact that we could not combine various dimensions, we chose to focus on categories only. *TCOF-POS* [BEN 12] is a freely available corpus[30] of French spontaneous speech annotated in POS. It was perfect for our experiment, as the corpus was pre-segmented and the annotators did not have to review this, but only to categorize the units. In addition, this annotation task did not generate significant prevalence. However, the used tagset contained a hierarchy of types (*PRO:ind*, *PRO:dem*, *PRO:cls*, etc.), which has to be taken into account.

The results that we obtained are shown in Figure 1.20. They confirm the ones we got from artificial annotations. The observed agreement, which does not take chance into

---

30 The corpus is available here: http://www.cnrtl.fr/corpus/perceo/.

account, this time under-estimates the agreement. The weighted kappa seems to be the metrics that underestimates the least agreement in this case. This metric was computed from a user-defined matrix of weights, deduced from the annotation guide. These weights take into account the fact that an error between two categories (two types) is more serious than that between a category and its sub-categories. For example, the weight associated with an error between the following two sub-categories *Verb-PPRES* and *Verb-FUTUR* of the same category (*Verb*) is 0.5, whereas the weight associated with an error between two categories, like *Verb-PPRES* and *Noun* would be 1.

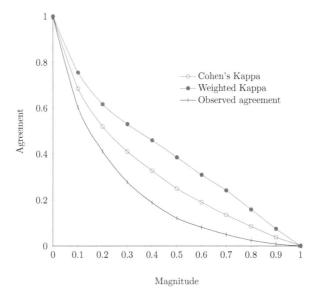

Figure 1.20. *Comparison of the behaviors of the metrics on categorization on the TCOF-POS corpus (no prevalence, but structure of the tagset taken into account). For a color version of the figure, see www.iste.co.uk/fort/nlp.zip*

Originally, the inter-annotator agreement on this corpus was computed using Cohen's kappa and reached 0.96. On the

Richter scale obtained using the `Corpus Shuffling Tool` and shown in Figure 1.20, this corresponds to a magnitude of 0.1, i.e. to a very limited deterioration. Therefore, we can say now without any doubt that the corpus is annotated in a very consistent way.

1.5. Conclusion

We covered here the bases for sound collaborative manual annotation: we detailled the annotation process, proposed a grid of analysis of the annotation complexity, gave an overview of the main annotation tools and exposed the potential biases in the annotation evaluation.

The next part of the book will be devoted to a major trend in NLP, crowdsourcing annotation. We will deconstruct the myths and show how reliable annotation can be obtain using ethical crowdsourcing.

2

Crowdsourcing Annotation

Crowdsourcing represents a dramatic evolution for language resource development and data production in general. Not only does the change in scale push to their limits the annotation methodologies and tools, but it also modifies our relationship, as researchers, to the citizens, who become our employees or our partners.

These specificities make it the perfect testbed for manual annotation "engineering".

2.1. What is crowdsourcing and why should we be interested in it?

2.1.1. *A moving target*

Defining the term "crowdsourcing" appears to be a research subject as such [EST 12]. As new applications appear, the definition evolves and revolves around the chosen focus. Rather than adding ours to the pile, we will comment on the most used definitions and give examples, going in depth to deconstruct the myths.

The term "crowdsourcing" was first coined by Jeff Howe of Wired Magazine as "the act of a company or institution taking a function once performed by employees and outsourcing it to an undefined (and generally large) network of people in the form of an open call" [HOW 06b]. The crowdsourced definition of crowdsourcing in Wikipedia is now that of the Merriam-Webster dictionary: "the practice of obtaining needed services, ideas, or content by soliciting contributions from a large group of people and especially from the online community rather than from traditional employees or suppliers".[1] But it used to be[2] closer to the original definition:

DEFINITION 2.1 (Crowdsourcing).– *"The act of outsourcing tasks, traditionally performed by an employee or contractor, to an undefined, large group of people or community (a crowd), through an open call".*

Anyway, two important differences are to be noted between Howe's definition and the others. First, Howe does not emphasize as much the number of participants. Second, using the term "network", he insists on the relationship between participants. We will soon see that his definition is closer to reality than that of Wikipedia and Merriam-Webster from those points of view.

Besides, Howe explicitly defines the source of the task to perform as "a company or institution", thus differentiating between "crowdsourcing" and "commons-based peer production" (also known as "social production") [HOW 06a], where the task can be initiated by anyone, like Wikipedia[3] or the Distributed Proofreaders[4] of the Gutenberg project. The importance given to the distinction for Howe is linked to his economic standpoint and seems somewhat artificial for our purpose. We will therefore consider "social

---

1 See: http://www.merriam-webster.com/dictionary/crowdsourcing.
2 Consulted on December 2, 2010.
3 See: https://en.wikipedia.org.
4 See: http://www.pgdp.net/.

production" as part of crowdsourcing rather than a distinct production mode.

Due to the instability in the definition, there are today many crowdsourcing taxonomies, many of which are presented in [GEI 11]. We will use the following two criteria to categorize crowdsourcing applications: (i) is the crowdsourced task remunerated (remuneration)? (ii) is the purpose of the task obvious to the participant (transparency)? Using this simplified grid of categorization and focusing on crowdsourcing for data production, a superset including annotation, we obtain three main types of crowdsourcing:

1) volunteer and transparent crowdsourcing, such as Wikipedia and Distributed Proofreaders;

2) remunerated and transparent crowdsourcing, which includes microworking crowdsourcing platforms like Amazon Mechanical Turk;

3) volunteer and non-transparent crowdsourcing, including GWAPs like JeuxDeMots and ZombiLingo.

The purpose of GWAPs can be to solve a problem or to create data, in our case it is to generate language data.

Obviously, as in any categorization process, there is a continuum here and a well-known GWAP for NLP like Phrase Detectives can prove difficult to categorize. First, it is more a gamified interface than a game, so the task is rather transparent, but it is presented in an indirect way. Second, players can win gift cards, which is not a remuneration, but still represents money. However, this is not the main motivation for playing and it is not emphasized as, for example, on Amazon Mechanical Turk. Despite its specifics, Phrase Detectives can therefore be included in the third category.

We will use examples from these three types of applications throughout this chapter to illustrate what can be expected from crowdsourcing from the annotation standpoint.

2.1.2. *A massive success*

Crowdsourcing is undoubtedly a massive success and it represents more than just a low-cost solution, a shift in power.

Started in 2001, the `Wikipedia` crowdsourced encyclopedia contains more than 30 million articles in more than 241 languages.[5] Its English version is accessed 8 million times an hour (800,000 for the French version).

The `Distributed Proofreaders` was created in 2000 to assist the `Project Gutenberg`[6] in providing and correcting digitized Public Domain books. The number of active proofreaders is around 1,000 (1,372 in February 2015, 1,209 in August 2015) and they proofread nearly 30,000 books[7] in seven languages (English, German, French, Italian, Portuguese, Spanish, Dutch).

The first well-known and advertised Game With A Purpose (GWAP, see section 2.3), the `ESP game`, proposed to players to tag images. The success was huge, with 13,500 participants tagging 1.3 million images in 3 months [AHN 06].

In a very different domain, French law imposes representatives to declare their conflicts of interest. They handed out unusable hand-written forms. The association `Regards Citoyens` (citizen watch) created an online

---

5 See: http://stats.wikimedia.org/EN/Sitemap.htm.
6 See: http://www.gutenberg.org/.
7 See: http://www.pgdp.net/c/stats/stats_central.php.

platform to digitize the scanned pdf files.[8] With a little advertisement in the press, 11,095 declaration extracts were digitized in less than a week by nearly 8,000 participants. The declarations are now searchable and were used by journalists to unveil misconducts.

2.2. Deconstructing the myths

2.2.1. *Crowdsourcing is a recent phenomenon*

The advent of the Web 2.0 in the 2000s has witnessed the multiplication of crowdsourcing activities, from the benevolent Wikipedia (2001), to the microworking platform Amazon Mechanical Turk (2005). However, the phenomenon is far from being recent. In particular, the scientific community did not wait for the Internet to become "social" to start using the power of the crowd through "citizen science".

A good example of this type of open call to perform science is the Longitude Prize, a £20,000 prize[9] awarded in 1714 by the British government to reward a simple and handy method to determine the longitude of a ship. The challenge still exists and in 2014 was focused on "Global antibiotics resistance". Another interesting example comes from the French National Museum (*Museum National d'Histoire Naturelle*), in Paris, which published in 1824 "Instructions for travelers and employees of the colonies" (*Instructions pour les voyageurs et les employés des colonies*, see Figure 2.1), a guide for non-academic travelers, explaining how to publicize their own experiments and observations in order for the scientific community to benefit from this work.

---

8 See: http://regardscitoyens.org/interets-des-elus/.
9 See: https://longitudeprize.org/.

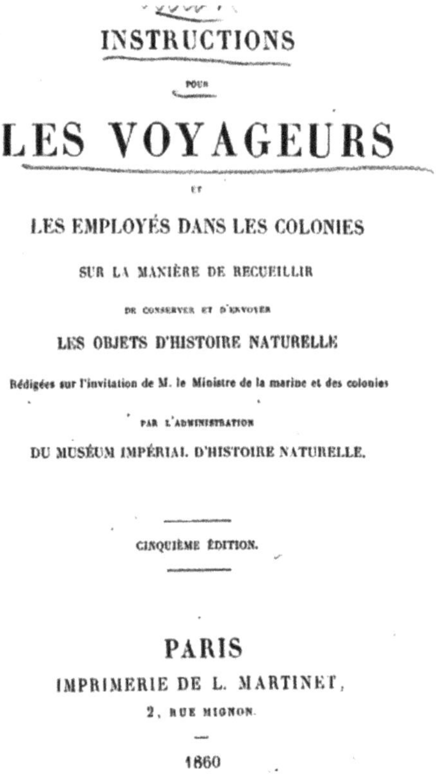

INSTRUCTIONS

POUR

LES VOYAGEURS

ET

LES EMPLOYÉS DANS LES COLONIES

SUR LA MANIÈRE DE RECUEILLIR

DE CONSERVER ET D'ENVOYER

LES OBJETS D'HISTOIRE NATURELLE

Rédigées sur l'invitation de M. le Ministre de la marine et des colonies

PAR L'ADMINISTRATION

DU MUSÉUM IMPÉRIAL D'HISTOIRE NATURELLE.

CINQUIÈME ÉDITION.

PARIS

IMPRIMERIE DE L. MARTINET,

2, RUE MIGNON.

1860

Figure 2.1. *Instructions for the travelers and employees of the colonies (French National Museum, 1860). The first edition dates from 1824*

Nevertheless, the Web represents a dramatic change in scale, allowing us to reach a potential of more than three billion people[10] with a click of a mouse. The evolution toward an interactive, "social" Web that we witnessed in the 2000s offers even more possibilities for crowdsourcing, as the users can now directly interact and participate in the project on the website.

---

10 See: http://www.internetlivestats.com/internet-users/.

2.2.2. *Crowdsourcing involves a crowd (of non-experts)*

This is reflected in the name itself: crowdsourcing implies a crowd (of participants). But what exactly is a crowd? and how many persons does it take to call it so? hundreds? dozens? more than ten? Although we can probably agree on the fact that less than a dozen is definitely not a crowd, the limit is hard to set.

According to the Merriam-Webster online dictionary,[11] a crowd is first "a large number of persons especially when collected together", which corresponds to the idea of a multitude, without defining what "a large number" is. The dozen most active participants in Phrase Detectives can hardly be considered a crowd (see Figure 2.2). However, the third sense of the word is "a group of people having something (as a habit, interest, or occupation) in common", a definition that focuses more on a common activity and less on the number of participants. This vision of the crowd corresponds precisely to what crowdsourcing is.

The "(out)sourcing" part of the term reflects the fact that the call to participants is open: anyone, with or without expertise in the domain, can participate. Obviously, this does not mean that everyone will. First, they have to know about the call, and second they have to be motivated to be part of it.

The reality of crowdsourcing practice is therefore far from what is being advertised. In Phrase Detectives, for example, although 2,000 persons registered as players between 2011 and 2012, only 13 created most of the annotations (see Figure 2.2) [CHA 13].

The same phenomenon appears on JeuxDeMots, with more than 1,200 players as a whole (see Figure 2.3)[12] and

---

11 See: http://www.merriam-webster.com/dictionary/crowd.
12 The numbers are regularly updated and available at: http://www.jeuxdemots.org/generateRanking-4.php?cat=scorests=1000td=allrd=10000.

ZombiLingo, with a total of 370 players (see Figure 2.4). The power law curve is typical of human activities. It also reflects the difference between advertising and reality. For example, Amazon Mechanical Turk announces a workforce of 500,000 Turkers (workers),[13] while we computed in [FOR 11a] that 80% of Amazon Mechanical Turk Human Intelligence Tasks (HITs) are completed by 3,011 to 8,582 Turkers, and that there are 15,059 to 42,912 Turkers in total.

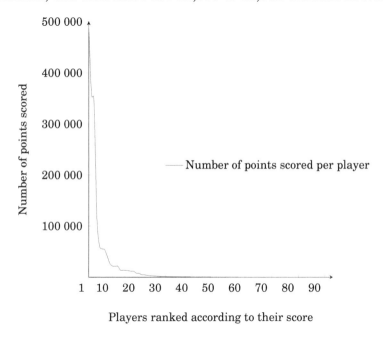

Players ranked according to their score

Figure 2.2. *Number of players on* Phrase Detectives *according to their scores (Feburary 2011 – Feburary 2012)*

The "crowd" in Amazon Mechanical Turk corresponds to the first sense of the word: a multitude of persons. However, the players on Phrase Detectives, JeuxDeMots and

13 See: https://requester.mturk.com/tour.

`ZombiLingo` can certainly be considered as a crowd because they engage in a common activity.

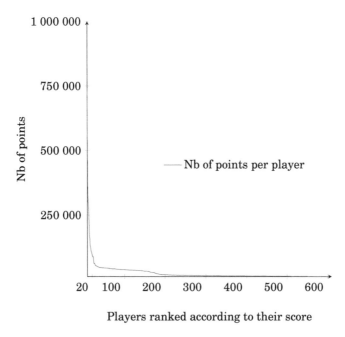

Figure 2.3. *Players on* `JeuxDeMots`

Participants in `Wikipedia` correspond to the same type of "common activity" crowd. The crowdsourced encyclopedia is, to our knowledge, the oldest online crowdsourcing application. As such, it offers a perspective on the functioning of such a system that no other application does. It is no surprise that the study of its participants shows more complex patterns.

The rise in the number of Wikipedia editors began slowly, with an acceleration from 2004 to 2007 (see Figure 2.5) to reach a peak at 56,400 active editors in 2007. It then began to decline steadily. This decline was attributed to an excess in rejection of contributions, leading to a drastic change "from 'the encyclopedia that anyone can edit' to the encyclopedia that anyone who understands the norms, socializes him or herself, dodges the impersonal wall of semi-automated rejection and still wants to voluntarily contribute his or her time and energy can edit" [HAL 13]. As of today, and for the English `Wikipedia`, the most important edits are from almost once in a lifetime editors,[14] and the most active editors mainly perform minor (but numerous) edits.

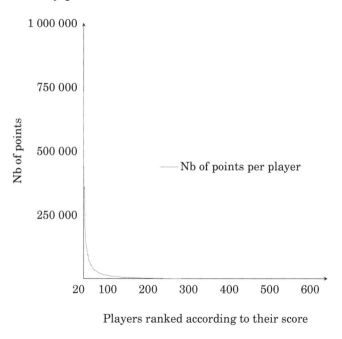

Figure 2.4. *Players on* `ZombiLingo`

One of the main issues with crowdsourcing systems is to manage to keep the momentum going: at least some of the newcomers should become the new "leaders", the new experts.

---

14 See: http://www.aaronsw.com/weblog/whowriteswikipedia.

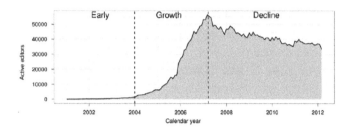

Figure 2.5. *Number of active, registered editors (>= 5 edits/month) in* Wikipedia *(Figure 1 from [HAL 13], courtesy of the author (CC-BY-SA))*

2.2.3. *"Crowdsourcing involves (a crowd of) non-experts"*

People participating in crowdsourcing activities are often referred to as "amateurs" or "non-experts", as opposed, for example in citizen science, to researchers or to traditionally employed people in agencies like the LDC[15] in the US or ELRA-ELDA[16] in France.

The definition of an expert, as given by the Merriam-Webster dictionary,[17] is the following: "one with the special skill or knowledge representing mastery of a particular subject". The definition of the adjective bears more informative power: "having, involving, or displaying special skill or knowledge derived from training or experience".

The question of the expertise of the annotators is one that regularly appears in research articles dealing with manual annotation, but is seldom considered as a subject as such. Authors write about "expert" annotators, sometimes opposing

---

15 See: https://www.ldc.upenn.edu/.
16 See: http://www.elra.info/en/.
17 See: http://www.merriam-webster.com/dictionary/expert.

them to "naive" or "non-expert" annotators (see for example [TEL 14]), without defining those terms, either because they seem obvious or because that would open the Pandora's box of acceptability judgments. Sometimes, more details are given concerning the annotators' background [PÉR 11] or they are defined as "domain experts" [CAN 14]. In rare cases, a very detailed description is given, like in [GEE 08]:

> "Naive annotators can be characterized as subjects that have not been linguistically trained but that have participated in an introductory session explaining the dialogue data, the dialogue act tagset, and the use of an annotation tool. Expert annotators can be characterized as linguistically trained subjects that have experience in annotating dialogue and are thoroughly familiar with the tagset."

However, this description is not linked to any general typology.

This ambiguity in the definition of the annotators' expertise is obvious in domains like biomedicine. A long discussion was held in October 2012 on the BioNLP mailing list[18] concerning the type of expert that would be the most efficient to annotate "linguistic" elements in a biomedical corpus, like named entities: a biomedical specialist or a linguist? To illustrate the issue, let us take the following (real) example from the French *Sequoia* corpus [CAN 12], which is manually annotated with constituents (syntax).

> "Pour les SCA, la durée de la perfusion dépend de la manière dont le SCA doit être traité: elle peut durer jusqu'à 72 heures au maximum chez les

---

18 The discussion title was: "Trends in Clinical NLP (Jon Patrick)".

patients devant recevoir des médicaments. (For the ACS (Acute Coronary Syndromes), the duration of the IV (intravenous drip) depends on the way the ACS should be treated: it can last a maximum of 72 hours for patients who need to take the drugs)."

Who would be an expert in this case? The sub-corpus (*EMEA*) is from the pharmacology domain and the annotation is of a certain type of linguistics (a certain type of syntax). Would you need a linguist? A pharmacist? Would a French-speaking person, without any specific knowledge in syntax or pharmacology, but trained for the task, be able to annotate (correctly) this type of sentence? If yes, would he/she be an expert or a non-expert (a naive annotator)?

It seems to us that it is crucial to distinguish between (i) the expertise of the domain of the corpus (here, pharmacology), (ii) the expertise of the annotation domain (here, a certain type of syntax) and (iii) the expertise of the task (here, annotating constituents with a certain tool, according to certain guidelines). In all cases, at the heart of expertise lies training.

The crowdsourcing participants who produce a lot of data do have experience and in many cases they are well-trained. We know that because we know that they produce quality data. In Phrase Detectives and in ZombiLingo, for example, the games include reference annotations which help evaluate the quality of the players' production. In Phrase Detectives, the accuracy of the players ranges from 0.7 to 0.8 when compared to experts of the annotation domain [CHA 09a]. However, the identification of "properties" resulted in a massive failure with an accuracy close to 0. In the following example, postman is a property of Jon:

EXAMPLE 2.1.– Jon, the postman, delivered the letter.

If we can consider that at least some players became experts in the anaphora annotation task as presented in `Phrase Detectives`, none of them managed to master the annotation of properties and become experts of the task. This is probably due to a lack of training, with the tutorial focusing on anaphora rather than properties.

In `ZombiLingo`, early results show an average of 0.86 accuracy for the 10 best players (removing the results from the best one and the worst one, see Table 2.1). The accuracy gets even better if we include all the players (around 0.9), but then the majority of the participants played only the easiest phenomena. It has to be noted, however, that these results underestimate the noise (identification of a phenomenon where there is none) produced in non-reference cases, due to a (still) badly designed interface. To attract the attention of the players on this, the tutorial has to include sentences without the phenomenon at hand, which we added in the new version.[19]

$Rank$	$Correct$	$Total$	%
1	1,702	1,785	95.35%
2	549	985	55.74%
3	807	909	88.78%
4	566	659	85.89%
5	477	517	92.26%
6	318	444	71.62%
7	296	382	77.49%
8	201	214	93.93%
9	195	213	91.55%
10	131	150	87.33%

Table 2.1. *Accuracy of the most productive players in* `ZombiLingo`

---

19 Version 2.0 was released mid-January 2016.

The players do manage to annotate dependency relations in domains like pharmacology, as they became experts of the annotation task (see Figure 2.6).

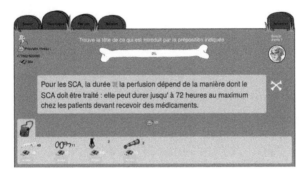

Figure 2.6. *Annotation of a dependency relation with* ZombiLingo *in the pharmacology domain: "For the Acute Coronary Syndroms (ACS), the duration of the IV depends on the way the ACS should be treated: it can last a maximum of 72 hours for patients who need to take drugs"*

If the training of the players is at the heart of GWAPs, especially for manual corpus annotation, it is not planned in microworking. In particular, platforms like Amazon Mechanical Turk do not provide for any specific means to train the workers (*Turkers*). The latter are at the mercy of wrongdoings from *Requesters* (persons proposing tasks) who can decide to exclude them without even having to justify this [FOR 11a]. *Turkers* therefore have to train by themselves on the task, without being remunerated. This generates a large amount of hidden work, as shown in [GUP 14].

On Amazon Mechanical Turk, *Turkers* can be awarded the distinction of *Masters*: "Workers achieve a Masters distinction by consistently completing HITs [tasks] of a certain type with a high degree of accuracy across a variety of requester [people proposing tasks]".[20] However, this

_____

20 See: https://www.mturk.com/mturk/help?helpPage=workerwhat_is_master_worker.

distinction is not awarded by *Requesters*,[21] who seem to favor the identification of their own experts, mainly because they do not have to pay them as much as Masters. Thus, some *Turkers* can probably be considered as experts, whether they are Masters[22] or not, as they specialized in one or several types of HITs.

As we already saw, the English Wikipedia, after a rise in edits from administrators, saw from 2004 an evolution toward more newcomers' edits until 2007, when the number of active editors began to slowly decrease (see Figure 2.5) [KIT 07]. These active editors now mainly perform the maintenance, clean-up and encyclopedian police work. They know their Five Pillars[23] by heart and enforce them with more or less patience. They are considered by some as Wikipedia's *bourgeoisie* [KIT 07].

The quality of Wikipedia is a field of research as such, of which an interesting state-of-the-art is not only presented in [CAL 10b], but also in Wikipedia itself.[24] More or less scientific studies were carried out, trying to compare the crowdsourced encyclopedia with, for example, the venerable Encyclopedia Britannica. Although it is much like comparing apples and oranges, as Wikipedia has a much wider coverage than the Britannica, the outcome is interesting: articles in Wikipedia show a great variety in length and readability, but the information they provide is correct overall. When comparable to the Britannica, the real issue lies in omission errors. Direct assessment methods were also developed (see, for example [VOS 05, HU 07,

---

21 See the point of view of *Requesters* on this: http://turkrequesters. blogspot.fr/2012/11/thought-masters-was-just-bad-for-non.html.
22 The real number of Masters is difficult to evaluate (it is probably less than advertised by Amazon).
23 See: https://en.wikipedia.org/wiki/Wikipedia:Five_pillars.
24 See: https://en.wikipedia.org/wiki/Reliability_of_Wikipedia.

CAL 10b]), including within Wikipedia itself.[25] This is a neverending issue, as Wikipedia evolves constantly and hopefully, thanks to the administrators' efforts, it is getting better. However, the best way to ensure its quality is to (stop complaining and) participate!

2.3. Playing with a purpose

Mathieu Lafourcade defines GWAP as games that are useful for a community (of researchers, for example) and real games for the players [LAF 15c]. This definition suggests that the players are only participating to play. This underestimates the importance given by some players in their participation in a scientific project (citizen science). We therefore prefer to give it a more open definition:

DEFINITION 2.2.– *A Game With a Purpose is an entertaining setting (a gamified interface, or a full-fledged game) in which voluntary participants produce data that require human knowledge and learning capabilities.*

The purpose of these games can vary, from problem solving (FoldIt) to language resource creation (JeuxDeMots, ZombiLingo).

A detailed list of games can be found in French in [LAF 15c]. This section is intended to show the possibilities offered by GWAPs, rather than list the existing ones. It therefore focuses on a limited number of examples.

Also, for the sake of analysis, games are classified into three groups, but there is obviously a continuum here, as, for example, all games imply some sort of training period. However, in some of them, the training concerns mainly the interface and the gameplay, while in others, it concerns the task itself.

---

25 See: https://en.wikipedia.org/wiki/Wikipedia:WikiProject_Wikipedia/ Assessment.

2.3.1. *Using the players' innate capabilities and world knowledge*

Using the innate capabilities and world knowledge of the players is the obvious way to go.

In the NLP field, JeuxDeMots[26] (see Figure 2.7) uses the players' ability to associate ideas to create a lexical network [LAF 08]. One player's associations of ideas are compared to another random player and points are gained only when they find identical terms, especially if the terms are new to the network. In this sense, it is a directly collaborative game, in which the participant knows with whom he/she has been compared.

Figure 2.7. *Interface of the game* JeuxDeMots: *give ideas associated with the following term: "Quality"*

The game allowed us to create more than 48 million relations in a network containing more than 800,000 terms and named entities.[27] More importantly, these relations are constantly updated and the resulting network can be freely downloaded at anytime.[28] This makes the created language

---

26 See (and play, in French): http://www.jeuxdemots.org.

27 These numbers are provided on the homepage of the game, as of January 10th, 2016.

28 Here, under a Public Domain license: http://www.jeuxdemots.org/JDM-LEXICALNET-FR/?C=M;O=D.

resource completely dynamic, a unique feature in the language resource world.

Another interesting characteristic of JeuxDeMots is that it is not just a gamified interface, but a fully-fledged game, with a rich long-lasting gameplay. Apart from the usual leader board and scored points, JeuxDeMots offers the player a whole range of interactions with others: possibility to challenge other players, to bring them to "justice" (lawsuits) when their games seem too badly played, to send "hot potatoes" or gifts, etc. According to its creator, Mathieu Lafourcade, most players in JeuxDeMots do not seem to care about the created language resource or the fact that they play to help researchers: they play simply because they like the thrill of the game.

Moreover, JeuxDeMots gave birth to a galaxy of smaller GWAPs, often voting games, that offer a useful distraction from the main game, while allowing us to enrich the produced language resource. As an example, LikeIt lets you vote on whether you like a term or not and see what the other players chose [LAF 15b].[29] The game allowed us to polarize 25,000 terms in three months with 150,000 votes. As a comparison, Polarimots [GAL 12], a polarized lexicon created manually by three linguists contains 7,473 words. One could think that the quality would differ, but a comparison shows that LikeIt agrees with Polarimots in almost 93% of the cases covered by the latter.[30] In addition, the resource created by LikeIt is dynamic and will therefore keep track of changes in polarity over time (for example, "terrific" used to be negative, as well as "trop" in French).

---

29 See (and play, in French): http://www.jeuxdemots.org/likeit.php.
30 See: http://www.jeuxdemots.org/data/eval_polarimot.php.

2.3.2. *Using the players' school knowledge*

Another possibility is to rely on the basic knowledge learned at school by the players.

This is what the designers of `Phrase Detectives`[31] did concerning grammar, in particular anaphora (or co-reference) resolution [CHA 08]. They built a gamified interface allowing the players to annotate the referent of a term (see Figure 2.8). The players are given detailed instructions and are briefly trained on the task, before they can actually annotate. This interface allowed us to produce a 200,000-word annotated corpus, with a relatively high level of quality (see section 2.2.3).

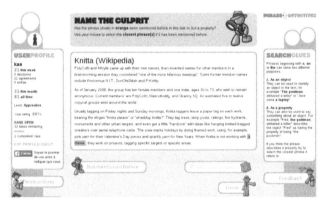

Figure 2.8. *Phrase Detectives: annotation interface*

`Phrase Detectives` alternates the annotation mode with a second playing mode, in which participants are asked to judge other players' annotations (see Figure 2.9). This peer validation adds a collaborative layer to the interface: an annotation is considered correct if enough participants agree on it. This collaboration is indirect, as the participant does

---

31 See: https://anawiki.essex.ac.uk/phrasedetectives/.

not know whose annotations they are correcting or agreeing with.

Figure 2.9. *Phrase Detectives: peer validation interface*

2.3.3. *Using the players' learning capacities*

As GWAPs proved their efficiency, people started looking beyond the already acquired capacities of the participants and considered training them on complex tasks. This is how another type of GWAP has emerged in the past few years, using the players' virtually endless learning capacities.

FoldIt[32] [KHA 11] is a perfect example of this type of GWAP: it helps players, without any prior knowledge in biochemistry, learn how to fold proteins [COO 10b]. Building upon the extraordinary innate 3D capabilities of human beings, the game includes a tutorial, broken down into concepts, with puzzles for each concept, giving access to the following puzzles only if the player has reached a sufficient level (see Figure 2.10).

---

32 See: http://fold.it/portal/.

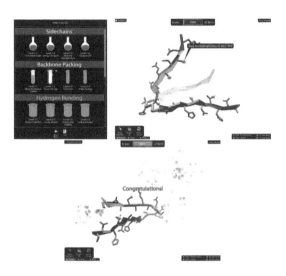

Figure 2.10. *FoldIt: game interface*

By playing FoldIt, a team of players found in a couple of weeks the solution to the crystal structure of a monomeric retroviral protease (simian AIDS-causing monkey virus), an issue which had remained unsolved for over a decade (see the progress of the team on Figure 2.11). This result could allow for the creation of antiretroviral drugs, an amazing outcome for a game!

More recently, we developed such a GWAP for dependency syntax annotation, a notoriously complex annotation task. The resulting game, ZombiLingo[33] [FOR 14b], allows players to learn to annotate syntactic phenomena while eating heads to become a more degraded zombie (see Figure 2.12). To do so, we first identified the complexity dimensions of the annotation task, following the complexity grid proposed in [FOR 12d] and presented in section 1.2. This led us to decompose the task into phenomena (dependency relations) instead of sentences and to propose a tutorial for each of them (see Figure 2.13). As

33 See: http://zombilingo.org/.

in `Phrase Detectives`, the players are not allowed to play a phenomenon until they reach a certain level of success during the tutorial.

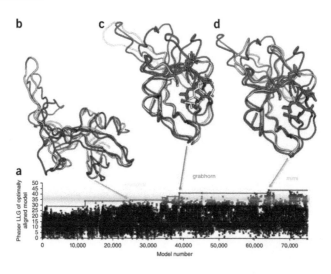

Figure 2.11. *FoldIt: progress of the team that found the solution (pseudos of the players are shown in colors). For a color version of the figure, see www.iste.co.uk/fort/nlp.zip*

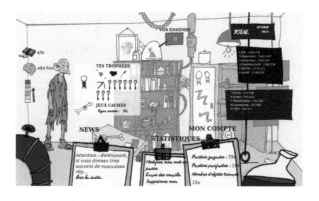

Figure 2.12. *ZombiLingo: a fully-fledged game for dependency syntax annotation (player's page)*

However, the training does not stop at the tutorial stage. Players are regularly proposed with reference sentences and if they do not annotate them properly, a correction is given; the level of confidence we place in the players is lowered and their chance to play another reference sentence is raised. Furthermore, they are warned that after three faulty annotations they will have to redo the tutorial on this phenomenon. We also offer the participants the possibility to retrain using the tutorial whenever they need (for example, after a long period without playing).

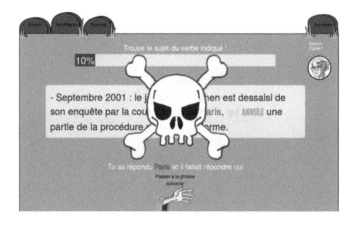

Figure 2.13. *ZombiLingo: tutorial interface (correction of an error)*

The input corpus is pre-annotated using a parser (for French, we used Talismane [URI 13]) and the pre-annotated relations are given a score of 5. The players confirm or correct the pre-annotations. Each time a player selects a relation, the score of this relation is increased by the level of the player and if the relation does not exist yet, it is initiated with the level of the player. For the moment, there is no real collaboration between players in the game as the participants do not know what the others are doing. However, they can question the answers which are given to them (in case of reference sentences) and we (the managers of the game) try to answer all of them (or to correct the reference, when the players are right). We plan to add more interactions in future versions of `ZombiLingo`, including a forum (attached to annotations, so that players can interact and correct themselves), a chat room and a challenge mode (where one player can challenge another on some sentences).

The quality of the obtained annotation, as evaluated on the reference sentences, is very high (see section 2.2.3) and even if we think it is a bit overrated, as reference sentences do contain the phenomenon, whereas the others do not, we think that this first version of `ZombiLingo` shows that it is possible to produce high quality complex annotations with a game. We are aware that there is room for improvement, but the first results are very promising from the quality point of view.

As for the produced quantity, it is simply astonishing! We obtained nearly 50,000 annotations in one month, produced by a total of approximately 300 players, with little publicity and still with a Beta version of the game. As of the end of January 2016, we reached more than 90,000 annotations by 580 players.

Those examples show that there is virtually no end in sight to what we can train people to do if we manage to make it fun. The limits are mainly that of our imagination and of our capacity to design games and to obtain the necessary technical means.

2.4. Acknowledging crowdsourcing specifics

2.4.1. *Motivating the participants*

A vital issue in crowdsourcing in general is to get a sufficient number of people to try and play or work, in order to gather a subgroup of highly productive participants. Motivation is therefore a key question, which is about convincing people not only to participate (motivation), but also to come back and participate again (volition [FEN 09]).

There exist several theories of motivation in the field of gamification, including the *GameFlow* theory [SWE 05], derived from the more general *Flow* theory, which dates from 1975 and is presented in detail in [NAK 02]. Mathieu Lafourcade used a much simpler and general grid for `JeuxDeMots`,[34] the CIA *MICE* framework for agent recruitment:[35] *Money, Ideology, Coercion, Ego*. Obviously, in crowdsourcing, the terms have to be adapted, and *Money* can also be reward (in games), *Ideology* can be considered in a wider, less political sense of interest (participating to science, for example), *Coercion* should obviously remain light (like a loss of points if the player does not come back when he/she is challenged by another player, or being forced to retrain after a number of errors); only *Ego* will not need to be adapted. This "grid" of analysis is a bit simplistic (as expressed in the CIA document, which presents a more complex model, *RASCALS*), but it represents an interesting first attempt at understanding the potential motivations of the players in the crowd.

Although *Ideology* is probably too strong a word to characterize it, people participating in citizen science do have an interest in helping researchers. Beyond that, participants in platforms like `Wikipedia` are encyclopedians and as such they participate in the transmission of knowledge [KIT 07], which can be considered as an ideal (if not ideology). Needless to say that there is not only one motivating factor for the participation in such a task and that *Ego* is probably a powerful trigger too.

Contrary to what is written in some papers, in particular in [SNO 08], social science studies have shown that workers in microworking platforms like `Amazon Mechanical Turk`

---

34 Personal communication, November 6th, 2013.
35 See "Burkett-MICE to RASCALS.pdf" in https://www.cia.gov/library/ center-for-the-study-of-intelligence/csi-publications/csi-studies/studies/vol.-57-no.-1-a/vol.-57-no.-1-a-pdfs.

are mainly motivated by the money they earn and that it is not a hobby for them [IPE 10a]. However, some difficulties encountered by researchers on the platform show that there are not enough *Turkers*. For example, the usual very low remuneration has proven not to be enough reward in some cases where the number of potential *Turkers* for a specific task is low: for the transcription of Korean, wages had to be increased from $5 to $35 per hour to get the task done [NOV 10]. Also, very large tasks can prove difficult to perform [IPE 10b]. In addition, the task payment logic induces a strong bias in favor of quantity rather than quality.

While most GWAPs do not propose any financial remuneration, some of them, including Phrase Detectives, offer an indirect financial incentive through regular lotteries (where each annotation has a chance to win) and prizes for high scoring players [CHA 13]. This mechanism is quite different from the microworking logic: the players are not remunerated for each task they perform. Instead, the randomness of the lotteries generates motivation even for players who do not play a lot. More importantly, remuneration is not placed at the heart of the system like in Amazon Mechanical Turk (see Figure 2.14), and enjoyment remains the main incentive for players to come and play.

However, the substance of enjoyment is difficult to capture with the *MICE* grid of analysis, which seems a bit too rough for that. A first step in understanding it is to try to classify the different types of participants. A well-known typology in the field of game design is that of Richard Bartle [BAR 96]. Bartle defined four main types of players (*Achievers*, *Killers*, *Socialisers*, *Explorers*), according to their interest in the game: *acting on* or *acting with* (interacting), with an emphasis put on the game itself (world) or the players (see Figure 2.15).

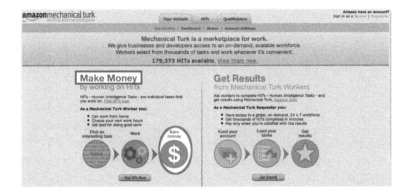

Figure 2.14. *Homepage of* `Amazon Mechanical Turk`*: remuneration is at the heart of the platform*

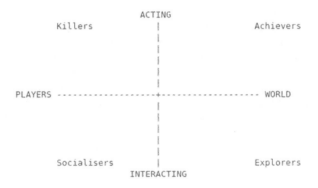

Figure 2.15. *Bartles Interest Graph [MAR 15]*

Achievers are interested in acting on the game, mastering it and its rules so well that they gain points more quickly than others. They represent the type of players everybody usually thinks of. The three other types are less obvious. For example, *Killers* are players who want to act on the other players, usually by attacking them. *Socialisers*, on the other hand, wish to interact with others, getting to know them and sharing tips with them. Finally, *Explorers* want to discover what is hidden in the game.

This inspired a more complex typology, which is presented on the `Gamified UK` website, the Marczewski's Player and User Types Hexad.[36] This model proposes four main types, *Achievers*, *Socialisers*, *Philanthropists* and *Free Spirits*, motivated respectively by *Relatedness*, *Autonomy*, *Mastery* and *Purpose* (see Figure 2.16). The first two types correspond more or less to Bartle's equivalent, while the *Free Spirits* category covers a bit more than the *Explorers* as *Free Spirits* want to explore or create, and *Philanthropists* are close to *Socialisers* while being more interested in the purpose of the game. The typology also contains two less positive types: *Players* (motivated by rewards) which are close to *Achievers* (motivated by mastery) and *Disruptors* (motivated by change), which are close both to *Killers* and *Explorers*.

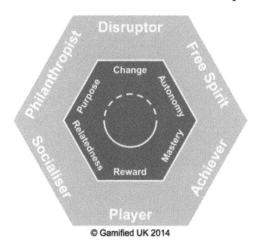

© Gamified UK 2014

Figure 2.16. *Marczewski's Player and User Types and Motivations Hexad, courtesy of the author [MAR 15]*

---

36 See: http://www.gamified.uk/user-types/.

Elements of gamification are added to the typology (see Figure 2.17). To attract many participants, a "good" game or gamified interface should satisfy each player type. Obviously, these typologies are not exhaustive and some players may be attracted by parts of the game that were not associated with motivating features. A good example is the phenomena page in ZombiLingo, in which the player can see, for each phenomenon, the number of played sentences and the number of remaining sentences: for some players (whom we could call *Collectors*), "finishing" a phenomenon is so satisfying that it makes them play more. We decided to take this into account and to find ways to improve the interface accordingly (changing the color of a finished phenomenon and putting it in a reserved place).

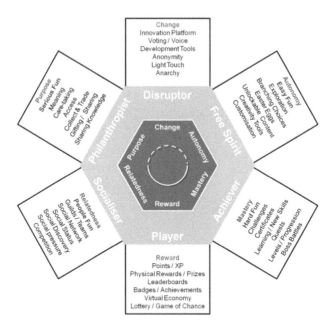

Figure 2.17. *Gamification elements according to player types, courtesy of the author [MAR 15]*

The best way to improve a GWAP is to play it and to take the players' remarks into account. Maintenance is therefore a key issue.

Attracting participants is the most important issue in crowdsourcing, as only a small proportion will contribute a lot to the data creation (see section 2.2.2). Advertising requires time and access to media, which is not always easy to obtain for researchers.

2.4.2. *Producing quality data*

Adding motivating game features should not impact the produced quality; on the contrary, it should have a positive effect on the quality. A player should score points only when he/she creates quality data (see Figure 2.18). However, preserving this virtuous circle is not always straightforward. Let us illustrate this with two examples from real game experiments.

Figure 2.18. *GWAP virtuous circle: the players should gain points only when they produce quality data*

In order to add fun to the game, we decided to add a feature to ZombiLingo: sentences disappearing randomly while playing. The players were surprised and this really added fun to the game, but when the sentence began disappearing, they tended to click at random, therefore creating a bad quality annotation. We quickly fixed this, deactivating the mouse click when the sentence started disappearing.

Another interesting anecdote concerns `JeuxDeMots`.[37] A player found a hack in the game to get more time to play (the game includes a timer). This player thus managed to create more data, quality data, which was good for the language resource creation perspective. However, this generated envy and anger in the community of players and was therefore bad for the game, so the player had to be banned.

More importantly, to be able to identify the degradation in quality we have to be able to evaluate this quality. Like in any other form of (non-crowdsourced) annotation, the evaluation means will depend on whether there is a reference or not.

If a reference exists, like in the case of `Phrase Detectives` or `ZombiLingo`, it can be used to evaluate the annotations produced by the participants, simply by comparing the produced result with the reference. This can (and should) be done on several occasions, not only during the training phase, to check that the players are still annotating correctly. In these GWAPs, players have to go through a training phase, during which all of their annotations are compared to the reference and feedback is given to them so that they understand and correct their errors (see for example Figure 2.13). They can progress in the tutorial and get to annotate non-reference sentences only if the results are correct enough, that is if they gave ten correct answers per phenomenon on `ZombiLingo` (indicated by a progress bar) or if 50% of their answers are correct in `Phrase Detectives` [CHA 13]. While playing, they will occasionally run into more reference sentences (without them knowing it) and receive feedback if their annotations are inconsistent with the reference ones. In `ZombiLingo`, the more wrong answers are given, the more likely the player will be exposed to reference sentences. This way, a very bad player will only play reference sentences and will either get better at it, or quit the

---

37 Mathieu Lafourcade, personal communication, July 11th, 2015.

game. The results of this evaluation can also be used to assign a confidence ranking to the players and to give them more "power" in the game, for example by trusting their annotations more or by giving them access to specific features, like challenges or hidden games.

If there is no reference available, the evaluation of the produced data should rely on other procedures. In the case of JeuxDeMots (which is strictly speaking not about annotating), Mathieu Lafourcade designed a "counter" game, TOTAKI,[38] to help in validating the created lexical network [LAF 15a]. The production of a GWAP can therefore be evaluated, at least partly, with another GWAP.

In the case of annotation, there is almost always a reference of some kind, at least a mini-reference (see section 1.1). However, this reference cannot help us in evaluating new annotations. We therefore need to use any evidence at our disposal. One of them is the level of confidence we have in the player, computed using the reference sentences (either during the training phase or after). Another one is the agreement between participants (vote), computed in a more or less complex way. In ZombiLingo, we decided to use a mix of the two and to give more importance to a vote from a player we trust more (see section 2.3.3).

2.5. Ethical issues

2.5.1. *Game ethics*

A well-known issue with games in general is that of addiction. It is however difficult to identify with online games, as even if we track the time spent by each player on the game, it only corresponds to the time between the player's

---

38 See: http://www.jeuxdemots.org/AKI2.php?thema=-1.

connection and logout, which is unrevealing, as first most players will not logout, and second we cannot know for sure they have been playing the whole time. Some games record the player's activity (directly or indirectly, like in JeuxDeMots, where the game is timed), but if there is no activity (mouse click or keyboard hit) it does not mean the player is not reflecting about an action in the game.

In addition, the limit between the temporary obsession with a game that most players have experienced and real addiction is difficult to identify. Although there is no real consensus over the definition, video game addiction seems to be revealed by three factors: (i) withdrawal symptoms, (ii) loss of control over gaming and (iii) conflict [KIN 13]. As GWAPs creators, we should be aware of the dangers of creating a game that is so motivating that people can get unhealthily addicted to it. The role we can play in preventing players from falling into addiction is limited, but we can at least give information about video game addiction and provide contact information for a national hotline like *Joueurs Info Service* in France.[39]

GWAPs for research purpoes are citizen science platforms. As such, transparency should be at the heart of the process and players should be associated with the project: information about it should be given, with links to publications and contact information of the researchers. If relevant, they can (should) be associated with publications. Also, what comes from the crowd should go to the crowd: linguistic resources created using GWAPs should be freely and directly available on the game website, at least for research purposes [LAF 14]. This means that the source corpora should be freely available as well.

---

39 See: http://www.joueurs-info-service.fr/.

Finally, the personal data gathered from the players, if any, should be treated with respect. They should never be given away and the collected data should obviously be limited to what is necessary for the game. If need be, the players who gave their email address can be contacted for further research questions, for example gender-related questions.

Information about all this should be presented in the game charter,[40] in which game-related rules can be added (for example the prohibition to sell assets gathered in the game).

2.5.2. What's wrong with Amazon Mechanical Turk?

Amazon Mechanical Turk (AMT) is a microworking platform, massively used in NLP, which clearly puts the emphasis on remuneration (see Figure 2.14). We already saw in section 2.4.1 that the most productive workers on this platform consider it as an important source of revenue. However, the proposed (micro)remunerations on Amazon Mechanical Turk are very low (we explain why in [FOR 11a]), US$1.25 an hour on average according to [ROS 10].

This is even more so as the Requesters (people proposing tasks) can simply refuse to pay the *Turkers* if they are not happy with the work performed, without even having to justify it (see Figure 2.19). This is a source of stress on the *Turkers'* side, which leads them to train on some tasks before officially (being registered) working on them, thus generating hidden unpaid work. This process is detailed in [GUP 14], which also shows the constraints the *Turkers* impose themselves in order to get interesting HITs, in particular sleep deprivation due to

---

40 See ZombiLingo's charter (in French) here (login first): http://zombilingo.org/compte/accueilCoIns#charte.

the time difference (most of the Requesters are from the US, while the *Turkers* studied in this article are located in India).

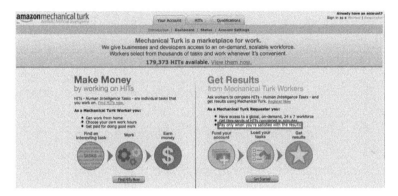

Figure 2.19. *Amazon Mechanical Turk:* "Pay only when you're satisfied with the results"

Furthermore, Amazon Mechanical Turk does not provide any means to equivalently ban *Requesters* responsible for wrongdoings.[41] The work relationship is therefore completely unbalanced. In addition, there is no direct link between *Turkers* and *Requesters*, as only Amazon.com has information about who is behind which pseudo. Moreover, *Turkers* are considered as independent workers, not employees. As such, they are supposed to pay taxes on their remunerations, which is doubtful given the very low amounts they earn. Due to the dilution of work, microworking crowdsourcing deprives states of income.

Some researchers in the NLP community reacted in favor of the *Turkers*. Apart from our efforts in explaining what AMT really is [FOR 11a], others tried to formalized good practices [ADD 13]. Finally, Chris Callison-Burch created a tool for the

---

41 The *Turkers* created tools like Turkopticon to try and counter this: https://turkopticon.ucsd.edu/login.

Turkers to be able to find higher paying HITs based on the hourly rate [CAL 14].

2.5.3. *A charter to rule them all*

We decided to go one step further and we imagined the Ethics and Big Data Charter as a tool to provide funding agencies with the necessary information they need to be able to make ethical choices when selecting projects. Another goal of this charter is to provide this information to all the potential users of a (language) resource. It was designed in collaboration with representatives from interest groups, private companies and academic organizations, including *ELDA*,[42] the French *CNRS*,[43] *ATALA*,[44] *AFCP*[45] and *APROGED*.[46]

We demonstrated the need for such a document in [COU 14]. Using the LRE map [CAL 12] as our main source, we showed that if the providers of language resources usually give details on the nature of the data and the persons to contact, they are not always explicit about the license (it is provided in only half of the cases) and even less so (a little more than 30%) about the status of the persons who created the resource (and whether it was through crowdsourcing or not) or on the quality assurance of the production.

The Ethics and Big Data Charter aims at addressing all these points in a single document, which, for practical

---

42 Evaluations and Language resources Distribution Agency, http://www.elda.org/.

43 Centre National de la Recherche Scientifique/National agency for scientific research, http://www.cnrs.fr/.

44 Association pour le Traitement Automatique des Langues/Natural Language Processing Association, http://www.atala.org.

45 Association Française de Communication Parlée/French spoken communication association, http://www.afcp-parole.org.

46 Association de la Maîtrise et de la Valorisation des contenus/Association for mastering and empowering content, http://www.aproged.org.

reasons, is self-administered. It is split into three major sections: (i) traceability, (ii) intellectual property and (iii) specific legal issues. The first part gives details on the participants of the project, their status and remuneration and the selection criteria. It also describes if and how the data were de-identified as well as the quality assurance procedures that were used, if any. The second part deals with license and copyright issues, particularly detailing cases where the language resource is created from one or several existing resources: for example, the *TCOF-POS* corpus [BEN 12], which was built upon the *TCOF* corpus. The third part is intended for country-specific legal requirements to be explained.

The charter is available as a pdf document[47] and will soon be provided as a Web form to be filled online. Our hope is that it would help favor projects implying participants who are treated fairly. For the moment, only the French funding agency *Cap Digital* included the Ethics and Big Data Charter in its grants proposal.

---

47 See, for English: http://wiki.ethique-big-data.org/chartes/charteethi queenV2.pdf.

Conclusion

Manual corpus annotation is now at the heart of NLP. It is where linguistics hides, in a still ill-explored way. There is a blatant need for manual annotation engineering (in the sense of a precisely formalized process), and this book aims at providing a first step toward a holistic methodology, with a global view on annotation.

Annotating is interpreting and this interpretation has to come from a consensus, built collaboratively. From this point of view, annotation is, by definition, collaborative and represents a shift from a vision according to which one specialist (a linguist) can make irrevocable judgments. There are many ways in which this collaboration can be fostered during the annotation process, and we detailed some of them in this book.

However, the annotation methodology is still little explored as such and many issues remain open. In particular, the annotation of relations and sets has to be analyzed more closely, as they represent a wide variety of situations and complexities. Also, better solutions still need to be found to evaluate them.

As we showed in Chapter 2, crowdsourcing is one of the most effective solutions to lower the cost of manual annotation. GWAP generates astonishing results, especially for language data production, both in terms of quantity and quality. However, designing and developing games require some specific gamification skills and technical expertise that are not accessible to everybody. Moreover, the necessary communication and the management of the community of players are time consuming, and a lot of researchers would rather avoid spending time on that.

Therefore, this solution can only be effective if a common platform is created, allowing researchers to generate small (for example, voting) games using simple online forms or more ambitious ones using the skills of specialized engineers. A community manager would take care of the community of players and of the communication concerning the games. Two platforms propose at least some of the necessary services: metadatagames,[1] which provides a gamified interface for collecting metadata, and Zooniverse, a freely accessible citizen science platform,[2] which is not gamified.

Crowdsourcing brings us closer to the people we work for as researchers. This highlights our responsibilities, as employers or partners, and should encourage us to be more ethical and transparent in our work.

---

1 See: http://www.metadatagames.org/.
2 See: https://www.zooniverse.org/.

Appendix

(Some) Annotation Tools

Keeping track of all the annotation tools is a job for Sisyphus. The list presented here is, therefore, far from exhaustive. It also contains deprecated tools or tools that were used only once, because they present interesting features that we want to expose. Finally, we have done our best to keep this list up-to-date, but some tools evolve so rapidly that it is difficult to keep track of changes; so if one of them seems interesting to you, do not hesitate to check its evolution on the provided website.[1]

We chose not to use the traditional comparative tabular presentation, as it does not allow for the representation of the different underlying principles behind each tool. We prefer to detail each of them in its context of creation and usage.

The organization of the inventory that we propose here relies on a typology that we deduced from our tests.[2] Thus, section A.1 presents generic tools, some of which were born so

---

1 Do not hesitate to contact us to bring a tool, a new feature or an error to our attention.

2 Note that most of these tests were done between 2010 and 2012. Since then, we have tried to keep track of the new systems but could not test all of them.

whereas others evolved toward from a specific annotation task. The following section logically introduces task-oriented tools. The annotation platforms, which aim more directly at applying NLP tools on corpora, are presented in section A.3. Finally, section A.4 details annotation campaign management tools. Within each section, the tools are presented in historical order, from the oldest to the newest.

A.1. Generic tools

The majority of the tools presented here were not initially designed to be generic, but were created for a specific task and were extended to other annotation tasks. They do not provide annotation management capabilities as such, but some of them include features like inter-annotator agreement computation.

A.1.1. *Cadixe*

Cadixe [ALP 04] is a deprecated annotation tool (the last version dates from March 2005), that is no longer available and we only list it here because it was used in the gene renaming campaign we mention in this book.

It provided a Java interface to add in-line XML tags to a corpus, from a DTD, with customized colors and styles, defined in a stylesheet (CSS, Cascading Style Sheet).

It was reasonably easy to use and reasonably documented, but with too limited features. In particular, the in-line format did not allow for the annotation of relations.

A.1.2. *Callisto*

Callisto [DAY 04] is freeware written in Java. It is "no longer actively supported",[3] but its source code is still available. The last version (1.8) dates from 2013. It was initially developed by the *MITRE Corporation*, with funding from the US Government.[4]

Callisto supports XML and generates standoff annotations following the ATLAS data model [BIR 00]. Interestingly, it allows importing and exporting in-line annotations.

Another interesting feature is that it relies on a modular and configurable architecture. It provides annotation services which are available to annotation modules. Some modules are already available, others can be developed. A module for temporal relations annotation was created (TANGO), but is no longer available.

Callisto is quite user-friendly if it is already configured for the planned annotation task (like anaphora resolution for example), but it is not easy to adapt to a new task.

New and interesting management features were planned (time tracking, inter-annotator agreement computation, etc.), but the last version is not documented and it is unclear whether they were actually added.

A.1.3. *Amazon Mechanical Turk*

Amazon Mechanical Turk[5] is now a very well-known microworking platform. It was first created by *Amazon.com*

---

3 See: https://github.com/mitre/callisto.
4 See: http://www.mitre.org/.
5 See: https://www.mturk.com.

for its internal needs. The firm opened the platform to other requesters in 2005.

Although it is not unique, this microworking platform is the most well-known and the most used, in particular in NLP. It allows *Requesters* to propose groups of simple tasks (*Human Intelligence Tasks* (HITs)) to be carried out by a large group of workers (*Turkers*). The real tasks are simplified so that they can be done by non-experts. For example, a "real" task related to recognizing textual entailment across several sentences that reflect either entailment, neutrality or contradiction might be simplified to the presentation of one pair of sentences and a binary response to a single question such as "would most people say that if the first sentence is true, then the second sentence must be true?" [BOW 15]. Execution of these simple tasks is paid for by the *Requesters*, provided that they are satisfied with the result. This is known as *artificial artificial intelligence*.

Amazon Mechanical Turk provides Web components that the *Requester* can use to present tasks to the Turkers in forms. A form contains one or more questions (explicit or implicit) to which the *Turker* must respond [SNO 08]. The "art" of the *Requesters* resides in their ability to decompose complex tasks, in particular annotation tasks (see, among many others, [SNO 08]) into simple (even simplified [BOW 15]) tasks and to adjust the remuneration, which is usually very low (for example, US$0.15 to identify a relation between two entities in a sentence).[6]

This system allows the production of very low-cost language resources ($1/10^{th}$ of the usual cost, at least

---

6 Found on February 10th, 2016 on the Amazon Mechanical Turk Web site.

according to [CAL 10a]), which explains, at least in part, its huge success in NLP over the course of the past 10 years.[7]

We showed the technical limits of this system in different position papers [FOR 11a, ADD 11], as well as in section 2.5.2, so we will not elaborate on them here. Further details concerning Amazon Mechanical Turk can be found in section 2.2.

Note that in some respects, Amazon Mechanical Turk is close to an annotation management tool: it differentiates between two roles (*Requester* and *Turker*); it provides some monitoring concerning the progression of the HITs, of the time spent on the tasks, and of the effective hourly pay rate; it distributes tasks to workers; and it manages the flow of the results. However, the scope of annotation management is much wider than the task management and includes versioning, evaluation tools, guidelines and corpus management (see section A.4).

A.1.4. *Knowtator*

Knowtator [OGR 06][8] is a free and open source Java plugin for the ontology editor Protégé,[9] which was originally developed for biomedical annotation. Its latest version dates from 2010, but it is still used on a number of annotation projects (for example, the CRAFT corpus [BRE 15]) involving an ontology.

Its backend code is directly inspired from that of WordFreak [MOR 03], and it allows for the standoff annotation of units and relations. It also offers a "consensus"

---

7 There are other reasons for this success, including the production speed, but most papers emphasize the cost.
8 See: http://knowtator.sourceforge.net/.
9 See: http://protege.stanford.edu/.

mode allowing the comparison and merging of annotations from several annotators.

Knowtator's annotations can be exported into any format supported by Protégé. However, it only accepts raw text as input and does not take into account existing XML tags. The tags are, therefore, visible and interfere with the text to annotate. Another limitation of this tool is that it is not compatible with the latest Protégé version.

A.1.5. *MMAX2*

MMAX2 [MÜL 06][10] is an open source Java program. It does not seem to be maintained anymore.

MMAX2 provides an integrated tokenizer. It supports XML and the annotations are standoff, which allows for the annotation of relations. It distinguishes between two types of relations: non-oriented relations (*sets*) and oriented relations (*pointers*). It also allows us to annotation discontinuities, partial overlaps and factorization.

Moreover, it allows us to add annotations from different levels in the same project, like *phrase*, *chunk* and *POS*. Finally, it offers a *AnnotationDiffWindow* plugin to visualize concurrent annotations of co-reference chains.

MMAX2 is, therefore, a richly featured tool, but it is difficult to use, due to a complex multi-windows interface. Like many other annotation tools, it gets really slow when the files are longer than a couple of pages. Finally, its documentation is limited.

---

10 See: http://mmax2.sourceforge.net/.

A.1.6. *UAM CorpusTool*

UAM CorpusTool [O'D 08] is an annotation tool originally designed for linguists, which is easy to install and configure. It is a Python program, which is only available for MS Windows and Mac OS. It is not open source, but it is free. It is still maintained, and a new version was released in November 2015.

UAM CorpusTool supports different linguistic annotation levels, the annotations are stored in standoff XML format, with one file per annotation level.

It is user-friendly and allows us to create annotation projects rapidly, through an interface dedicated to the organization of the corpus files and the creation of the annotation scheme. It allows to modify the annotation scheme during the project and to add glosses to each note.

It provides a powerful search engine (using CQL), that supports lexical patterns and searches through several levels of annotation. Automatic pre-processing is also available (sentence segmentation, chunking, POS annotation and syntactic taggins) as well as various statistical results.

However, the tool does not distinguish between roles (for example, manager and annotators). It also suffers from significant limitations: it is not possible to annotate relations, no *Undo* command is available.

A.1.7. *Glozz*

Glozz [WID 09] was created for the *Annodis* project, which aimed at creating a reference French corpus for discourse analysis. It is a generic tool, with specific features for discourse annotation (like a general view of the text being annotated). It is a freely available (for research) Java program.[11]

Glozz takes text as input and provides standoff annotations in XML. Its point-and-click interface is user-friendly and includes a customizable stylesheet to parameterize tags colors. Interestingly, it offers a *glue note* mode to add free comments. It also allows to hide some annotations (for example, POS when annotating named entities).

Its generic meta model proposes three types of components: *units* (adjacent textual elements), *relations* (binary relation between two units) and *schemas* (complex textual configuration including units and relations). Pre-annotations can be integrated, but they have to be standoff and to comply with this meta model.

Glozz includes a powerful search engine allowing us to search both the text and the annotations, with *GlozzQL*, a specific query language. It also provides the possibility to compute the inter-annotator agreement using γ [MAT 15], which is very useful.

However, Glozz is still not very robust (like many annotation tools) and becomes very slow with large files (more than a couple of hundred kilobytes).

A.1.8. *CCASH*

CCASH (*Cost-Conscious Annotation Supervised by Humans*) [FEL 10] is, as stated in its name, a cost-oriented annotation tool. It was designed to integrate automatic processing, such as tag dictionary [CAR 10], to limit the work of the annotators and to track the cost of annotation. Interestingly, this cost is

---

11 See: http://www.glozz.org/.

not only evaluated through the time spent on the task but also in terms of the number of interactions needed to perform an action.

It is a Web application, which can handle several annotators in parallel. It includes a limited administration interface, allowing an administrator to create annotation tasks and to assign them to users.

Annotations are standoff which allows for the annotation of relations. CCASH is highly flexible and customizable by developers, as it is open source.[12] A minimal documentation is available,[13] and the tool is still maintained and improved.

A.1.9. *brat*

BRAT (*brat rapid annotation tool*) [STE 12][14] was originally designed as an extension for an annotation visualization tool. It is now a very specific, fully collaborative annotation tool.

It is an active and maintained open source Web application, with a server written in Python and a CGI interface. Annotations are standoff.

BRAT provides a user-friendly interface allowing us to annotate both units and relations. An important feature of the tool is that each annotation is associated with a unique URL, which makes it one of the few tools supporting linked data.

Another specific of BRAT is the fact that it is fully and directly collaborative: annotators can work on the same corpus or the same document simultaneously and visualize

---

12 See: http://sourceforge.net/projects/ccash/.
13 See: https://facwiki.cs.byu.edu/nlp/index.php/CCASH.
14 See: http://brat.nlplab.org/index.html.

the modifications made by the others while they are added (this corresponds to the collaborative mode in SYNC3). In this tool, direct collaboration is not an option, it is the rule.

In the same spirit, the tool does not distinguish between roles and does not provide inter-annotator agreement metrics. However, it is possible to configure it to track the time spent on a document or on each editing and categorizing action.

For the moment, it is fully supported only on Chrome and Safari Web browsers, but it seems to work fine on Firefox too.

A.2. Task-oriented tools

An annotation tool is usually developed for a specific task. We present here some of the most well-known and some of the most original.

A.2.1. *LDC tools*

The LDC[15] has developed a number of tools to annotate speech and text, based on the AGTK, which instantiates a formalism derived from the annotation graphs [BIR 01]. These tools are all freely available and open source.[16]

AGTK is a set of software that can be used to develop annotation tools and which includes APIs allowing to manipulate annotation graphs as well as specialized graphical components.

These tools are detailed in [MAE 04] and include a transcription tool (XTrans), a tool dedicated to named entity annotation for the ACE campaign, tools allowing us to compare and adjudicate concurrent annotations.

---

15 See: http://www.ldc.upenn.edu/.
16 See: https://www.ldc.upenn.edu/language-resources/tools.

More recently, they developed a Web application (in PHP), the ACK [MAE 06] for simple annotation campaigns.

The LDC chose to specialize tools and to use a common formalism. This choice allows for a great flexibility and adaptability to the needs of each campaign, but it implies to develop new components regularly.

A.2.2. *EasyRef*

EasyRef [CLE 08] is a collaborative syntactic annotation tool. It was designed for the PASSAGE project (the acronym means "producing large scale syntactic annotations"), which planned the manual annotation of 500,000 French words to serve as reference for the systems participating to the project.

Since several teams from different locations were to use it, it was developed as a Web application. It still exists, is running and its main creator, Eric de la Clergerie, is planning to make it open source.

EasyRef[17] allows us to:

– visualize the annotations;

– add and edit annotations while preserving a precise trace of the modifications: each edit action creates a new version of the sentence, with an incremented revision number;

– check the syntactic coherence of the annotation by applying constraints;

– manage bug reports related to a sentence, including with discussions concerning a specific bug;

– search the annotations with regular expressions and administrative criteria (presence/absence of a bug report for example).

---

17 See: http://atoll.inria.fr/easyrefpub/login.

The traceability and collaboration features offered by `EasyRef` make it a very specific, very original tool that should inspire the next generation of annotation tools.

A.2.3. *Phrase Detectives*

`Phrase Detectives` [CHA 08][18] is a Web application designed for the manual annotation of anaphora. Its form is somewhat specific, as it is a gamified interface, a Game With A Purpose (GWAP, see section 2.3). The application itself is not freely available.

The texts proposed for annotation are automatically pre-annotated with the following pipeline of tools [KRU 09]: normalization, tokenization, parsing (with the Berkeley parser) and identification of the markables.

On `Phrase Detectives`, the players (the detectives) have to go through a training phase, playing on reference sentences. When they make an error, feedback is given to help them improve their understanding of the task. Once they reach a sufficient level, they can start playing, i.e. annotating for real. The game includes two modes: one in which they have to select the antecedent of the highlighted element in the text and another in which they have to validate annotations that were added by others.

Players gain points if other players agree with them. They are also regularly evaluated on the reference corpus. Several incentives are proposed to motivate players: a leaderboard, levels (and associated avatars), funny corpora (which the players can choose from) and vouchers for the best player and for a randomly picked annotation [CHA 09b]. Although the vouchers cannot be considered as remuneration *per se* and are not so much emphasized on the Web site, they still represent a step aside from citizen science.

---

18 See and play here: https://anawiki.essex.ac.uk/phrasedetectives/.

`Phrase Detectives` allowed us to annotate approximately 200,000 tokens, with satisfactory quality (see section 2.3).

This type of tool could probably be adapted to other annotation tasks involving (at least) binary relations, but as we already said, it is not available.

A.2.4. *ZombiLingo*

`ZombiLingo` [FOR 14b][19] is a GWAP designed for dependency syntax annotation. It is a Web application written in PHP, and it is meant to become open source as soon as the code is stabilized enough. It could probably be adapted to different sorts of binary relations annotations.

The game is presented in detail in section 2.3.3.

A.3. NLP annotation platforms

The main advantage of these platforms is that they provide access to NLP tools, such as tokenizers, POS taggers, chunkers or named entity extractors. These tools can be used for automatically pre-annotating the corpus. However, when these platforms support manual annotation, it is only a marginal feature, often added late (GATE) or still in development (UIMA).

A.3.1. *GATE*

GATE [CUN 02] (*General Architecture for Text Engineering*) is an open source platform developed by the University of Sheffield.[20] It provides access to existing NLP tools and resources and to develop new tools. In order to do this, GATE is a manual annotation interface (GATE Developer). The platform offers maintained (version 8.1 was released in June

---

19 See and play here: http://zombilingo.org.
20 See: http://gate.ac.uk/.

2015), documented and dedicated training, and even certification is provided.

As the tool was primarily designed for automatic processing rather than for manual annotation, the annotation interface remained poorly documented until version 5. Dedicated efforts have been made to document the following versions of the interface, but manual annotation in GATE remains marginal and limited to the correction of automatic annotations. A simple test shows that it is still impossible to undo an action. Also, the original text can (also) easily be modified, which generates errors, in particular when comparing annotations.[21]

Still, GATE provides a wide choice of useful options, such as toggling a source document between editable and uneditable states (*Read Only*). The annotator can also create new categories for manual annotation (*Restricted/Unrestricted annotation set*). The ANNIE module (*A Nearly New Information Extraction System*) proposes a number of useful automatic processing: sentence segmentation, tokenization, POS tagging and named entity recognition (using gazetteers). Finally, rules can be written with JAPE (Java Annotation Patterns Engine).

Features of GATE, while not always easy to handle, are varied and numerous. For example, the annotator can automatically annotate all the occurrences of a same term in a text (*annotate all*); visualizing annotation and searching in the text are easily performed; GATE includes an editor for co-reference chains.

Supported input formats include raw text as well as major markup languages (XML and HTML). The annotations are standoff in the TIPSTER [GRI 98] format and are stored

---

21 This, among others, is reported here: http://mpqa.cs.pitt.edu/annotation/gate_basics/.

either as a relational database or as a file (XML or Java serialization). In addition, GATE provides an API to the applications it proposes and is embedded in UIMA.

GATE includes a nice interface to activate or not and to compare annotations from different annotators (the Annotation Diff tool). The agreement can be defined more or less leniently. However, the inter-annotator agreement measurement is for the moment restricted to the coefficients of the kappa family and the F-measure.

The GATE team has recently released Teamware [BON 10] for the management of annotation campaigns which is further presented in section A.4.

A.3.2. *EULIA*

EULIA [ART 04] is a Web-based collaborative annotation tool dedicated to linguistic analysis. It inputs and outputs XML TEI documents and manipulates feature structures. The annotations are standoff. In addition to providing an environment for annotation, EULIA includes a search engine and also NLP tools for tokenizing, POS tagging and chunking.

The annotation of relations is apparently not possible. EULIA is not open source and is apparently no longer maintained.

A.3.3. *UIMA*

The goal of the *Apache* UIMA[22] (*Unstructured Information Management Applications*) project is to support the development of an architecture and applications for the processing of unstructured (text) information. Initially

---

22 See: http://uima.apache.org/.

developed by *IBM* [FER 04], Apache UIMA is embedded in the Eclipse IDE.

The effort required to install the environment is compensated by the large number of off the shelf *annotators* (automatic annotation tools) including a space-based tokenizer, a stemmer (Snowball), a HMM-based POS tagger, a regular expressions based annotation tool, a named entity extractor (OpenCalais) and a dictionary compiler to identify predefined text segments. Any other available tool can be installed.

The CAS Editor provides basic features for the manual annotation of texts. The annotation of relations cannot be performed with its interface. It is somewhat complex to install, even though it is provided as an Eclipse plugin since UIMA version 2.3.0. As far as we know, the CAS Editor has not yet been used for a fully-fledged manual corpus annotation campaign.

A.3.4. *SYNC3*

SYNC3 [PET 12] is designed to support collaborative annotation. This open source software is freely available under a LGPL license, as part of the Ellogon[23] NLP platform.

SYNC3, though it is a collaborative tool, is not a Web application but a desktop application which synchronizes with a central server and stores documents and metadata in a database. This original approach is, according to the designer, justified, as it caters for a richer user interface (possibility to define keyboard shortcuts or launch local treatments, advanced customization, etc.) while allowing annotators to work offline.

---

23 See: http://www.ellogon.org/.

SYNC3 exposes Ellogon features such as computation of inter-annotator agreement, but does not provide any specific user interface to manage annotation or user rights.

Interestingly, the tool induces customizable regular expressions from recorded annotations to automatically annotate text segments.

SYNC3 supports two annotation modes: distributed and collaborative. In the former, annotators work on different versions of the document while in the latter, all the annotators work on the same document, in a way similar to brat (see section A.1.9). In the "collaborative" mode, all the annotations are stored.

A.4. Annotation management tools

There are only few real annotation management tools. They are more or less available and their features can differ, but they have in common to be much more than an annotation interface and to support the whole campaign process and not only the annotation.

A.4.1. *Slate*

Slate [KAP 10, KAP 12] (*Segment and Link-based Annotation Tool Enhanced*)[24] is a very complete annotation management tool. It is now open source and freely available.[25] It is a Web application, with a Java server and an annotation interface in Flash. Slate is, therefore, very visual, very pleasing to use for an annotator, but requires the Flash player. It supports Chrome and Safari, but not Firefox (like BRAT).

---

24 See: http://www.cl.cs.titech.ac.jp/slate.

25 The source code can be found here: https://bitbucket.org/dainkaplan/ slate/overview.

In Slate, there are two types of users, the *administrators* and the *annotators*. The administrator can create annotation projects, manage the users, assign annotation tasks (and remove them), monitor the progression of the work, and import and export data. The administrator is provided with an interface highlighting the differences between parallel annotations and allowing to merge them to create a reference.

Slate offers the possibility to version the annotation project, much like a standard development project. All the annotation instances are identified with the version number of the project, hence of the tagset, at the time of its annotation. From our point of view, this is essential. Note that this system is different from that implemented in BRAT, as the versioning allows us to link the tagset (and the guidelines) to the annotations.

Interestingly, in Slate, the administrator cannot annotate. As for the annotators, they cannot see the work carried on by others. The two roles are, therefore, completely independent.

In Slate, an annotation is a note, added either on a span of text or on a relation between spans of text (*links*). The relations can be oriented or not. The schema creation is flexible and multiple annotations can be added on a text span with any number of name/value attributes.

Slate generalizes a powerful feature of EasyRef: it allows us to define constraints on the annotation of segments and relations.

It also allows for the addition of new annotation layers, with new tagsets, referencing the previous layers. The created annotations are obviously standoff.

However, Slate does not provide any way of computing the inter-annotator agreement or to see the time spent by annotators on their task.

A.4.2. *Djangology*

Djangology [APO 10] is a Web-based annotation management tool written in Python using the Django framework.[26] It is intended to be easy to install and to allow for distributed and collaborative annotation of text documents. It is freely available and open source[27] and seems little maintained (the last modification in the source code dates from 2010). The documentation is very limited too.

From the annotation management point of view, Djangology provides an administration interface allowing us to manage documents and users and to define the data model for the annotation. It also proposes an interface to compare parallel annotations and to compute basic inter-annotator agreement metrics.

As an annotation tool, Djangology offers basic annotation capabilities, including the automatic propagation of annotations (the equivalent of *Annotate all* in GATE). It does not seem to allow to annotate relations.

A.4.3. *GATE Teamware*

GATE Teamware [BON 10] is an extension of GATE (see section A.3.1) designed for organizing and performing online "collaborative" annotation. Like GATE, Teamware is open source (under an Affero GPL license) and freely available.[28]

The architecture of the tool is described in [BON 10]. It distinguishes between three processing layers: SOAP services for data storage, Web interfaces and an execution layer managing the flow of annotation projects. Interestingly, like

---

26 See: https://www.djangoproject.com/.
27 See: http://sourceforge.net/projects/djangology/.
28 See: https://gate.svn.sourceforge.net/svnroot/gate/teamware/trunk/.

in SYNC3, the annotation tool is a locally installed software, while the Web interface is used for campaign management.

Like Slate, Teamware makes an explicit distinction between the various roles of an annotation campaign. However, Slate acknowledges two types of actors, the *administrator* and the *annotators*, where Teamware supports three: *annotation managers, editors* or curators (experts) and *annotators*.

Curators measure inter-annotator agreements, carry out the adjudication, are in charge of the training of the annotators and answer their questions. The campaign managers define new annotation projects, monitor their progression, participate in the methodological choices (inter-annotator agreement computation, use of pre-annotation tools, etc.). Annotators are "non-experts" who have to be trained at the beginning of the campaign. The communication between the annotators and the editors is supported through instant messages. This organization is close to the one we propose (see section 1.1).

Teamware offers the same automatic annotation services as GATE, and its annotation interface is more or less the same. Similarly to Knowtator (see section A.1.4), Teamware supports the use of an ontology for annotation. An adjudication interface is provided to the editors, which allows them to select the annotations the best annotations among the ones proposed by the annotators. Finally, the campaign manager interface offers the possibility to create corpora, define the annotation scheme, configure pre-annotations and execute them on the corpora. It also allows us to monitor the campaign: progression (number of annotated documents, remaining to annotate and being annotated) and statistics concerning the annotators (time spent on a document, effective working time and inter-annotator agreement).

The application itself and the user rights are managed via two roles, *administrator* and *super administrator*.

This tool is very complete, but it presents the same usability issues as GATE. Finally, as for all the other Web-based annotation tools, it does not support Firefox.

A.4.4. *WebAnno*

WebAnno [CAS 14] is an annotation management tool that uses BRAT visualization and edition engine. It, therefore, provides the same annotation interface and is not supposed to work on Firefox. It supports Chrome and Safari. It is open source and freely available under the Apache Software License (ASL) version 2.[29] It proposes a test mode, with an embedded database, that is very useful for testing purposes.

WebAnno distinguishes between three roles, which are very similar to that of Teamware: *project manager*, *annotators* and *curators*, with the corresponding interfaces. Unlike in BRAT, annotators cannot directly collaborate on a document, as they work separately.

It supports the annotation of relations and chains (in particular, coreference chains) and provides basic sentence segmentation and tokenization. It also offers the possibility to lock/unlock the tagset. Interestingly, it provides a left-to-right/right-to-left option, in order to be able to annotate right-to-left languages like Arabic. It supports a large variety of import and export formats.

WebAnno uses the DKPro Statistics library to compute inter-annotator agreement metrics. By default, it provides

---

29 See: https://webanno.github.io/webanno/.

Cohen's kappa, but the upcoming version 3 should include multiple metrics and parameters, as well as export in CSV format.[30]

A.5. (Many) Other tools

Many other annotation tools are available, but most of them are not usable (for different reasons) or no longer available.

PALinkA [ORA 03] seems to have disappeared. The same goes for Serengeti [STÜ 07]. It seems that CSAF [KIM 12] does not exist anymore. TextAE is an "embeddable visual editor of text annotation".[31] It is usually coupled with the PubAnnotation repository.[32] It was designed for community-based annotation in the biomedical domain; it is open source and freely available.

As for Annotatornia [PRZ 09], if it is still available[33] and is open source under a Mozilla Public License, it does not seem to be maintained anymore. Moreover, its interface and documentation only exist in Polish. To our knowledge, it is the only annotation tool written in Ruby.

WordFreak [MOR 03] is an open source Java-based annotation tool, available under the Mozilla Public License.[34] It is no more maintained, but it inspired a number of current annotation tools.

ANALEC [LAN 12] is a very interesting and original Java tool, which is compatible with Glozz. It offers specific visualization features and geometric analyses. It is still

---

30 Richard Eckart de Castilho, personal communication, February 4th, 2016.
31 See: http://textae.pubannotation.org/.
32 See: http://pubannotation.org/.
33 Here: http://zil.ipipan.waw.pl/Anotatornia.
34 Here: http://wordfreak.sourceforge.net.

maintained, but is only provided and documented in French.[35]

Egas [CAM 14] proposes interesting features as an annotation management tool, but it is provided only as a Web service.

---

35 See: http://www.lattice.cnrs.fr/Telecharger-Analec.

Glossary

Annotation: covers both the process of adding a note on a source signal and the whole set of notes or each note that results from this process, without *a priori* presuming what would be the nature of the source (text, video, images, etc.), the semantic content of the note (numbered note, value chosen in a reference list or free text), its position (global or local) or its objective (evaluation, characterization, simple comment).

Crowdsourcing: "the act of outsourcing tasks, traditionally performed by an employee or contractor, to an undefined, large group of people or community (a crowd), through an open call" [Wikipedia, December 2, 2010].

Game With A Purpose: an entertaining setting – a gamified interface or a full-fledged game – in which voluntary participants produce data that require human knowledge and learning capabilities.

Markables: segments of the source signal that could be annotated: for example, all of the tokens for POS annotation, but only the noun phrases for named entity annotation.

Microworking: (micro) remunerated crowdsourcing, in which the tasks are decomposed and simplified so as to be carried out by workers, (micro) paid by the (micro) task.

Prevalence: a category is prevalent when it is dominant, i.e. when it is used more than the others, without the proportion being very precisely defined.

Requester: a person (or group of persons) proposing tasks on `Amazon Mechanical Turk`.

Turker: a worker on `Amazon Mechanical Turk`.

Bibliography

[ADD 11] ADDA G., SAGOT B., FORT K. *et al.*, "Crowdsourcing for language resource development: critical analysis of Amazon Mechanical Turk overpowering use", *Language and Technology Conference (LTC)*, Poznań, Pologne, p. 5, 2011.

[ADD 13] ADDA G., MARIANI, J.-J., BESACIER L. *et al.*, "Economic and ethical background of crowdsourcing for speech", *Crowdsourcing for Speech Processing: Applications to Data Collection, Transcription and Assessment*, pp. 303–334, Wiley, 2013.

[AHN 06] VON AHN L., "Games with a purpose", *IEEE Computer Magazine*, vol. 39 pp. 96–98, 2006.

[AKR 91] AKRICH M., BOULLIER D., "Le mode d'emploi, genèse, forme et usage", *Savoir faire et pouvoir transmettre*, pp. 113–131, Editions de la MSH (collection Ethnologie de la France, Cahier 6), 1991.

[ALE 10] ALEX B., GROVER C., SHEN R. *et al.*, "Agile corpus annotation in practice: an overview of manual and automatic annotation of CVs", *Fourth Linguistic Annotation Workshop (LAW)*, Association for Computational Linguistics, pp. 29–37, 2010.

[ALL 08] ALLAUZEN A., BONNEAU-MAYNARD H., "Training and evaluation of POS taggers on the French MULTITAG corpus", *Proceedings of the Sixth International Conference on Language Resources and Evaluation (LREC'08)*, Marrakech, Morocco, 28-30, European Language Resources Association (ELRA), available at: http://www.lrec-conf.org/proceedings/lrec2008/, May 2008.

[ALP 04] ALPHONSE E., AUBIN S., BESSIÈRES P. *et al.*, "Event-based information extraction for the biomedical the CADERIGE project", *JNLPBA COLING 2004 Workshop*, 2004.

[APO 10] APOSTOLOVA E., NEILAN S., AN G. *et al.*, "Djangology: a light-weight web-based tool for distributed collaborative text annotation", *International Conference on Language Resources and Evaluation (LREC)*, European Language Resources Association (ELRA), 19-21, May 2010.

[ART 04] ARTOLA X., DE ILARRAZA A.D., EZEIZA N. *et al.*, "EULIA: a Graphical Web Interface for Creating, Browsing and Editing Linguistically Annotated Corpora", *International Conference on Language Resources and Evaluation (LREC) Workshop on XML-based richly annotated corpora*, 2004.

[ART 08] ARTSTEIN R., POESIO M., "Inter-coder agreement for computational linguistics", *Computational Linguistics*, vol. 34, no. 4, pp. 555–596, MIT Press, 2008.

[BÖH 01] BÖHMOVÁ A., HAJIČ J., HAJIČOVÁ E. *et al.*, "The Prague Dependency Treebank: three-level annotation scenario", in ABEILLÉ A. (ed.), *Treebanks: Building and Using Syntactically Annotated Corpora*, Kluwer Academic Publishers, 2001.

[BAK 98] BAKER C.F., FILLMORE C.J., LOWE J.B., "The Berkeley FrameNet Project", *Annual Meeting of the Association for Computational Linguistics (ACL) and International Conference on Computational Linguistics (ICCL)*, ACL'98, Stroudsburg, PA, USA, Association for Computational Linguistics, pp. 86–90, 1998.

[BAK 10] BAKHOUCHE B., BEYS B., DELATTRE D. *et al.*, "De l'annotation aux marginalia", available at: http://meticebeta.univ-montp3.fr/lelivre/partie2/de_lannotation_aux_marginalia.html, 2010.

[BAR 96] BARTLE R., "Hearts, clubs, diamonds, spades: players who suit MUDs", *The Journal of Virtual Environments*, vol. 1, no. 1, 1996.

[BAR 10] BARQUE L., NASR A., POLGUÈRE A., "From the Definitions of the Trésor de la Langue Française to a Semantic Database of the French Language", *14th EURALEX International Congress*, 2010.

[BAY 11] BAYERL P.S., PAUL K.I., "What determines inter-coder agreement in manual annotations? A meta-analytic investigation", *Computational Linguistics*, vol. 37, no. 4, pp. 699–725, MIT Press, 2011.

[BEC 11] BECK K., "Manifesto for Agile Software Development", available at: http://agilemanifesto.org/, 02 2011.

[BEN 12] BENZITOUN C., FORT K., SAGOT B., "TCOF-POS: un corpus libre de français parlé annoté en morphosyntaxe", *Traitement Automatique des Langues Naturelles (TALN)*, Grenoble, France, pp. 99–112, 2012.

[BES 09] BESTGEN Y., "Quels indices pour mesurer l'efficacité en segmentation thématique?", *Traitement Automatique des Langues Naturelles (TALN)*, Senlis, France, p. 10, 2009.

[BHA 10] BHARDWAJ V., PASSONNEAU R., SALLEB-AOUISSI A. et al., "Anveshan: a tool for analysis of multiple annotators' labeling behavior", *Fourth Linguistic Annotation Workshop (LAW IV)*, 2010.

[BIR 00] BIRD S., DAY D., GAROFOLO J.S. et al., "ATLAS: a flexible and extensible architecture for linguistic annotation", *International Conference on Language Resources and Evaluation (LREC)*, ELRA, pp. 1699–1706, 2000.

[BIR 01] BIRD S., LIBERMAN M., "A formal framework for linguistic annotation", *Speech Communication*, vol. 33, no. 1/2, pp. 23–60, 2001.

[BOH 13] BOHNET B., BURGA A., WANNER L., "Towards the annotation of Penn TreeBank with information structure", *Proceedings of the Sixth International Joint Conference on Natural Language Processing*, Asian Federation of Natural Language Processing, pp. 1250–1256, 2013.

[BON 05] BONNEAU-MAYNARD H., ROSSET S., AYACHE C. et al., "Semantic annotation of the French Media Dialog Corpus", *InterSpeech*, 2005.

[BON 10] BONTCHEVA K., CUNNINGHAM H., ROBERTS I. *et al.*, "Web-based collaborative corpus annotation: requirements and a framework implementation", in WITTE R., CUNNINGHAM H., PATRICK J. *et al.* (eds), *Workshop on New Challenges for NLP Frameworks (NLPFrameworks 2010)*, ELRA, May 2010.

[BOW 15] BOWMAN S.R., ANGELI G., POTTS C. *et al.*, "A large annotated corpus for learning natural language inference", *arXiv Preprint arXiv:1508.05326*, 2015.

[BRE 15] BRETONNEL COHEN K., VERSPOOR K., FORT K. *et al.*, "The Colorado Richly Annotated Full Text (CRAFT) corpus: multi-model annotation in the biomedical domain", *Handbook of Linguistic Annotation*, 2015.

[BUR 12] BURGHARDT M., "Usability recommendations for annotation tools", *Proceedings of the Sixth Linguistic Annotation Workshop*, Association for Computational Linguistics, pp. 104–112, 2012.

[CAL 10a] CALLISON-BURCH C., DREDZE M., "Creating speech and language data with Amazon's Mechanical Turk", *CSLDAMT'10: Proceedings of the NAACL HLT 2010 Workshop on Creating Speech and Language Data with Amazon's Mechanical Turk*, Morristown, NJ, USA, Association for Computational Linguistics, 2010.

[CAL 10b] CALZADA G.D.L., DEKHTYAR A., "On measuring the quality of Wikipedia articles", *4th International Workshop on Information Credibility on the Web Proceedings*, pp. 11–18, 2010.

[CAL 12] CALZOLARI N., GRATTA R.D., FRANCOPOULO G. *et al.*, "The LRE Map Harmonising Community Descriptions of Resources", *Proceedings of the Eight International Conference on Language Resources and Evaluation (LREC)*, Istanbul, Turkey, pp. 23–25, May 2012.

[CAL 14] CALLISON-BURCH C., "Crowd-workers: aggregating information across turkers to help them find higher paying work", *The Second AAAI Conference on Human Computation and Crowdsourcing (HCOMP-2014)*, November 2014.

[CAM 14] CAMPOS D., LOURENÇO J., MATOS S. *et al.*, "Egas: a collaborative and interactive document curation platform", *Database*, June 2014.

[CAN 12] CANDITO M., SEDDAH D., "Le corpus Sequoia: annotation syntaxique et exploitation pour l'adaptation d'analyseur par pont lexical", *Traitement Automatique des Langues Naturelles (TALN)*, Grenoble, France, 2012.

[CAN 14] CANDITO M., PERRIER G., GUILLAUME B. *et al.*, "Deep syntax annotation of the sequoia french treebank", *Proceedings of the Ninth International Conference on Language Resources and Evaluation (LREC 2014)*, May 2014.

[CAR 96] CARLETTA J., "Assessing agreement on classification tasks: the kappa statistic", *Computational Linguistics*, vol. 22, pp. 249–254, 1996.

[CAR 10] CARMEN M., FELT P., HAERTEL R. *et al.*, "Tag dictionaries accelerate manual annotation", *International Conference on Language Resources and Evaluation (LREC)*, European Language Resources Association (ELRA), pp. 19–21, May 2010.

[CAS 14] DE CASTILHO R.E., BIEMANN C., GUREVYCH I. *et al.*, "WebAnno: a flexible, web-based annotation tool for CLARIN", *Proceedings of the CLARIN Annual Conference (CAC) 2014*, Utrecht, Netherlands, CLARIN ERIC, Extended abstract, October 2014.

[CHA 08] CHAMBERLAIN J., POESIO M., KRUSCHWITZ U., "Phrase detectives: a web-based collaborative annotation game", *Proceedings of the International Conference on Semantic Systems (I-Semantics'08)*, 2008.

[CHA 09a] CHAMBERLAIN J., KRUSCHWITZ U., POESIO M., "Constructing an anaphorically annotated corpus with non-experts: assessing the quality of collaborative annotations", *Proceedings of the 2009 Workshop on The People's Web Meets NLP: Collaboratively Constructed Semantic Resources*, People's Web '09, Stroudsburg, PA, USA, Association for Computational Linguistics, pp. 57–62, 2009.

[CHA 09b] CHAMBERLAIN J., POESIO M., KRUSCHWITZ U., "A new life for a dead parrot: incentive structures in the phrase detectives game", *Proceedings of WWW*, 2009.

[CHA 13] CHAMBERLAIN J., FORT K., KRUSCHWITZ U. *et al.*, "Using games to create language resources: successes and limitations of the approach", in GUREVYCH I., KIM J. (eds), *The People's Web Meets NLP, Theory and Applications of Natural Language Processing*, pp. 3–44, Springer Berlin Heidelberg, 2013.

[CHU 88] CHURCH K.W., "A stochastic parts program and noun phrase parser for unrestricted text", *Proceedings of the Second Conference on Applied Natural Language Processing*, ANLC '88, Stroudsburg, PA, USA, Association for Computational Linguistics, pp. 136–143, 1988.

[CHU 11] CHURCH K., "A Pendulum Swung Too Far", *Linguistic Issues in Language Technology LiLT*, vol. 6, 2011.

[CIM 03] CIMIANO P., HANDSCHUH S., "Ontology-based linguistic annotation", *Proceedings of the ACL 2003 Workshop on Linguistic Annotation*, Morristown, NJ, USA, Association for Computational Linguistics, pp. 14–21, 2003.

[CLE 08] DE LA CLERGERIE E.V., "A collaborative infrastructure for handling syntactic annotations", *First International Workshop on Automated Syntactic Annotations for interoperable Language Resources*, 2008.

[COA 92] COATES-STEPHENS S., "The analysis and acquisition of proper names for the understanding of free text", *Computers and the Humanities*, vol. 26, nos. 5–6, pp. 441–456, 1992.

[COH 60] COHEN J., "A coefficient of agreement for nominal scales", *Educational and Psychological Measurement*, vol. 20, no. 1, pp. 37–46, 1960.

[COH 68] COHEN J., "Weighted kappa: nominal scale agreement with provision for scaled disagreement or partial credit", *Psychological Bulletin*, vol. 70, no. 4, pp. 213–220, 1968.

[COH 05] COHEN K.B., FOX L., OGREN P.V. *et al.*, "Corpus design for biomedical natural language processing", *Proceedings of the ACL-ISMB Workshop on Linking Biological Literature, Ontologies and Databases: Mining Biological Semantics*, pp. 38–45, 2005.

[COL 88] COLOMBAT B., "Présentation: Eléments de réflexion pour une histoire des parties du discours", *Langages*, vol. 23, no. 92, pp. 5–10, Armand Colin, 1988.

[COO 10a] COOK P., STEVENSON S., "Automatically identifying changes in the semantic orientation of words", in CHAIR N. C.C., CHOUKRI K., MAEGAARD B. *et al.* (eds), *International Conference on Language Resources and Evaluation (LREC)*, 19-21, May 2010.

[COO 10b] COOPER S., TREUILLE A., BARBERO J. *et al.*, "The challenge of designing scientific discovery games", *Proceedings of the Fifth International Conference on the Foundations of Digital Games*, FDG '10, New York, USA, ACM, pp. 40–47, 2010.

[COU 14] COUILLAULT A., FORT K., ADDA G. *et al.*, "Evaluating corpora documentation with regards to the ethics and big data charter", *International Conference on Language Resources and Evaluation (LREC)*, Reykjavik, Islande, May 2014.

[CUN 02] CUNNINGHAM H., MAYNARD D., BONTCHEVA K. *et al.*, "GATE: a framework and graphical development environment for robust NLP tools and applications", *Proceedings of the 40th Anniversary Meeting of the Association for Computational Linguistics*, Philadelphia, USA, 2002.

[DAN 09] DANDAPAT S., BISWAS P., CHOUDHURY M. *et al.*, "Complex linguistic annotation – no easy way out! A case from Bangla and Hindi POS labeling tasks", *Proceedings of the Third ACL Linguistic Annotation Workshop*, 2009.

[DAV 82] DAVIES M., FLEISS J.L., "Measuring agreement for multinomial data", *Biometrics*, vol. 38, no. 4, pp. 1047–1051, 1982.

[DAY 04] DAY D., MCHENRY C., KOZIEROK R. *et al.*, "Callisto: a configurable annotation workbench", *International Conference on Language Resources and Evaluation*, 2004.

[DEN 09] DENIS P., SAGOT B., "Coupling an annotated corpus and a morphosyntactic lexicon for state-of-the-art POS tagging with less human effort", *Pacific Asia Conference on Language Information and Computing (PACLIC)*, 2009.

[DES 98] DESROSIÈRES A., *The Politics of Large Numbers: a History of Statistical Reasoning*, Harvard University Press, Cambridge, MA, 1998.

[DES 02] DESROSIÈRES A., THÉVENOT L., *Les catégories socio-professionnelles*, 5th ed., La Découverte, Paris, 5e edition, 2002.

[DES 14] DESROSIÈRES A., DIDIER E., "Prouver et gouverner: une analyse politique des statistiques publiques", *Sciences humaines, La Decouverte*, 2014.

[DIE 04] DI EUGENIO B., GLASS M., "The kappa statistic: a second look", *Computational Linguistics*, vol. 30, no. 1, pp. 95–101, MIT Press, 2004.

[DIP 04] DIPPER S., GÖTZE M., STEDE M., "Simple annotation tools for complex annotation tasks: an evaluation", in WITT A., HEID U., THOMPSON H.S. *et al.* (eds), *International Conference on Language Resources and Evaluation (LREC) Workshop on XML-based richly annotated corpora (XBRAC)*, 2004.

[EST 12] ESTELLÉS-AROLAS   E.   GONZÁLEZ-LADRÓN-DE GUEVARA F., "Towards an integrated crowdsourcing definition", *Journal of Information Science*, vol. 38, no. 2, pp. 189–200, 2012.

[FEL 98] FELLBAUM C., *WordNet: An Electronic Lexical Database*, MIT Press, 1998.

[FEL 10] FELT P., MERKLING O., CARMEN M. *et al.*, "CCASH: A Web Application Framework for Efficient, Distributed Language Resource Development", *International Conference on Language Resources and Evaluation (LREC)*, European Language Resources Association (ELRA), 19-21, May 2010.

[FEN 09] FENOUILLET F., KAPLAN J., YENNEK N., "Serious games et motivation", *4ème Conférence francophone sur les Environnements Informatiques pour l'Apprentissage Humain (EIAH09)*, vol. *Actes de l'Atelier Jeux Sérieux: conception et usages*, pp. 41–52, 2009.

[FER 04] FERRUCCI D., LALLY A., "UIMA: an architectural approach to unstructured information processing in the corporate research environment", *Natural Language Engineering*, vol. 10, pp. 327–348, Cambridge University Press, 2004.

[FLE 71] FLEISS J.L., "Measuring nominal scale agreement among many raters", *Psychological Bulletin*, vol. 76, no. 5, pp. 378–382, 1971.

[FOR 09] FORT K., EHRMANN M., NAZARENKO A., "Towards a methodology for named entities annotation", *3rd ACL Linguistic Annotation Workshop (LAW III)*, pp. 142–145, 2009.

[FOR 10] FORT K., SAGOT B., "Influence of pre-annotation on POS-tagged corpus development", *Fourth ACL Linguistic Annotation Workshop*, pp. 56–63, 2010.

[FOR 11a] FORT K., ADDA G., COHEN K.B., "Amazon Mechanical Turk: gold mine or coal mine?", *Computational Linguistics (editorial)*, vol. 37, no. 2, pp. 413–420, 2011.

[FOR 11b] FORT K., NAZARENKO A., RIS C., "Corpus linguistics for the annotation manager", *Corpus Linguistics Conference*, p. 13, 2011.

[FOR 12a] FORT K., Les ressources annotées, un enjeu pour l'analyse de contenu: vers une méthodologie de l'annotation manuelle de corpus, PhD thesis, University Paris XIII, LIPN, INIST-CNRS, 2012.

[FOR 12b] FORT K., CLAVEAU V., "Annotating football matches: influence of the source medium on manual annotation", *International Conference on Language Resources and Evaluation (LREC)*, p. 6, May 2011.

[FOR 12c] FORT K., FRANÇOIS C., GALIBERT O. et al., "Analyzing the impact of prevalence on the evaluation of a manual annotation campaign", *International Conference on Language Resources and Evaluation (LREC)*, p. 7, May 2012.

[FOR 12d] FORT K., NAZARENKO A., ROSSET S., "Modeling the complexity of manual annotation tasks: a grid of analysis", *International Conference on Computational Linguistics (COLING)*, pp. 895–910, 2012.

[FOR 14a] FORT K., ADDA G., SAGOT B. et al., "Crowdsourcing for language resource development: criticisms about amazon mechanical turk overpowering use", in VETULANI Z., MARIANI J., (eds), *Human Language Technology Challenges for Computer Science and Linguistics*, pp. 303–314, Springer International Publishing, July 2014.

[FOR 14b] FORT K., GUILLAUME B., CHASTANT H., "Creating zombilingo, a game with a purpose for dependency syntax annotation", *Gamification for Information Retrieval (GamifIR'14) Workshop*, Amsterdam, Netherlands, April 2014.

[FOR 14c] FORT K., GUILLAUME B., STERN V., "ZOMBILINGO: eating heads to perform dependency syntax annotation (ZOMBILINGO: manger des têtes pour annoter en syntaxe de dépendances)", *Proceedings of TALN 2014 (Volume 3: System Demonstrations)*, Marseille, France, Association pour le Traitement Automatique des Langues, pp. 15–16, July 2014.

[FRU 12] FRUNZEANU E., PONS P., "Les "encyclopédies" médiévales et les digital humanities: l'évolution du programme Sourcencyme", *Journée d'étude sur l'annotation collaborative de corpus*, 2012.

[GAL 12] GALA N., BRUN C., "Propagation de polarités dans des familles de mots : impact de la morphologie dans la construction d'un lexique pour l'analyse d'opinions", *Actes de Traitement Automatique des Langues Naturelles (TALN 2012)*, Grenoble, 2012.

[GEE 08] GEERTZEN J., PETUKHOVA V., BUNT H., "Evaluating dialogue act tagging with naive and expert annotators", *Proceedings of the Sixth International Conference on Language Resources and Evaluation (LREC'08)*, Marrakech, Morocco, 28-30, European Language Resources Association (ELRA), Available at: http://www.lrec-conf.org/proceedings/lrec2008/, May 2008.

[GEI 11] GEIGER D., SEEDORF S., SCHULZE T. *et al.*, "Managing the crowd: towards a taxonomy of crowdsourcing processes", *AMCIS 2011 Proceedings*, 2011.

[GOE 10] GOECKE D., LÜNGEN H., METZING D. *et al.*, "Different views on markup", in WITT A., METZING D., IDE N. (eds), *Linguistic Modeling of Information and Markup Languages*, vol. 40 of *Text, Speech and Language Technology*, pp. 1–21, Springer Netherlands, 2010.

[GRE 97] GREEN A.M., "Kappa statistics for multiple raters using categorical classifications", *Proceedings of the Twenty-Second Annual Conference of SAS Users Group*, San Diego, USA, 1997.

[GRI 96] GRISHMAN R., SUNDHEIM B., "Message Understanding Conference-6: a Brief History", *The 16th conference on Computational linguistics*, Morristown, NJ, USA, Association for Computational Linguistics, pp. 466–471, 1996.

[GRI 98] GRISHMAN R., TIPSTER Architecture Design Document Version 3.1, Report, DARPA, 1998.

[GRO 11] GROUIN C., ROSSET S., ZWEIGENBAUM P. *et al.*, "Proposal for an extension of traditional named entities: from guidelines to evaluation, an overview", *5th Linguistic Annotation Workshop*, Portland, Oregon, USA, pp. 92–100, 2011.

[GUP 14] GUPTA N., MARTIN D., HANRAHAN B.V. *et al.*, "Turk-Life in India", *Proceedings of the 18th International Conference on Supporting Group Work*, GROUP '14, New York, USA, ACM, pp. 1–11, 2014.

[GUT 04] GUT U., BAYERL P.S., "Measuring the reliability of manual annotations of speech corpora", *Speech Prosody*, pp. 565–568, 2004.

[GWE 12] GWET K.L., *Handbook of Inter-rater Reliability*, Advanced Analytics, LLC, third edition, 2012.

[HAB 05] HABERT B., "Portrait de linguiste(s) à l'instrument", *Texto!*, vol. X, no. 4, 2005.

[HAL 13] HALFAKER A., GEIGER R.S., MORGAN J. *et al.*, "The Rise and Decline of an Open Collaboration System: How Wikipedias reaction to sudden popularity is causing its decline", *American Behavioral Scientist*, vol. 57, no. 5, pp. 664–688, December 2013.

[HEL 13] HELLMANN S., LEHMANN J., AUER S. *et al.*, "Integrating NLP using linked data", *Proceedings of the 12nd International Semantic Web Conference (ISWC)*, Springer, 2013.

[HON 11] HONG J., BAKER C.F., "How good is the crowd at "real" WSD?", *Proceedings of the 5th Linguistic Annotation Workshop*, Portland, Oregon, USA, Association for Computational Linguistics, pp. 30–37, 2011.

[HOV 10] HOVY E.H., LAVID J.M., "Towards a "Science" of corpus annotation: a new methodological challenge for corpus linguistics", *International Journal of Translation Studies*, vol. 22, no. 1, 2010.

[HOW 06a] HOWE J., "Crowdsourcing: a definition", available at: http://crowdsourcing.typepad.com/cs/2006/06/crowdsourcing_a. html, 2006.

[HOW 06b] HOWE J., "The rise of crowdsourcing", *Wired Magazine*, vol. 14, no. 6, 06 2006.

[HRI 02] HRIPCSAK G., HEITJAN D.F., "Measuring agreement in medical informatics reliability studies", *Journal of Biomedical Informatics*, vol. 35, no. 2, pp. 99–110, Elsevier Science, 2002.

[HRI 05] HRIPCSAK G., ROTHSCHILD A.S., "Agreement, the F-measure, and reliability in information retrieval", *Journal of the American Medical Informatics Association (JAMIA)*, vol. 12, no. 3, pp. 296–298, 2005.

[HU 07] HU M., LIM E.-P., SUN A. *et al.*, "Measuring article quality in Wikipedia: models and evaluation", *Proceedings of the Sixteenth ACM Conference on Conference on Information and Knowledge Management*, CIKM '07, New York, USA, ACM, pp. 243–252, 2007.

[IDE 06] IDE N., ROMARY L., "Representing linguistic corpora and their annotations", *International Conference on Language Resources and Evaluation (LREC)*, 2006.

[IDE 07] IDE N., SUDERMAN K., "GrAF: A graph-based Format for linguistic annotations", *Linguistic Annotation Workshop, held in conjunction with ACL 2007*, pp. 1–8, 2007.

[IDE 08] IDE N., BAKER C., FELLBAUM C. *et al.*, "MASC: the manually annotated sub-corpus of American English", *International Language Resources and Evaluation (LREC)*, European Language Resources Association (ELRA), 28-30, May 2008.

[IPE 10a] IPEIROTIS P., "Mechanical turk requester activity: the insignificance of the long tail", available at: http://behind-the-enemy-lines.blogspot.com/2010/10/mechanical-turk-requester-activity.html, 2010.

[IPE 10b] IPEIROTIS P., "The new demographics of mechanical turk", available at: http://behind-the-enemy-lines.blogspot.com/2010/03/new-demographics-of-mechanical-turk.html, 2010.

[JOU 11] JOURDE J., MANINE A.-P., VEBER P. *et al.*, "BioNLP Shared task 2011 – bacteria gene interactions and renaming", *BioNLP Shared Task 2011 Workshop*, Portland, Oregon, USA, Association for Computational Linguistics, pp. 65–73, 2011.

[JUR 09] JURAFSKY D., MARTIN J.H., *Speech and Language Processing (2nd Edition)*, Prentice-Hall, Inc., Upper Saddle River, NJ, USA, 2009.

[KAI 08] KAISSER M., LOWE J.B., "Creating a research collection of question answer sentence pairs with Amazon's Mechanical Turk", *International Conference on Language Resources and Evaluation (LREC)*, 2008.

[KAP 10] KAPLAN D., IIDA R., TOKUNAGA T., "Annotation process management revisited", *International Conference on Language Resources and Evaluation (LREC)*, pp. 365–366, May 2010.

[KAP 12] KAPLAN D., IIDA R., NISHINA K. *et al.*, "Slate – a tool for creating and maintaining annotated corpora", *Journal for Language Technology and Computational Linguistics*, vol. 26, no. 2, pp. 89–101, 2012.

[KHA 11] KHATIB F., DIMAIO F., COOPER S. *et al.*, "Crystal structure of a monomeric retroviral protease solved by protein folding game players", *Nature Structural & Molecular Biology*, vol. 18, no. 10, pp. 1175–1177, Nature Publishing Group, 2011.

[KIM 08] KIM J.-D., OHTA T., TSUJII J., "Corpus annotation for mining biomedical events from literature", *BMC Bioinformatics*, vol. 9, no. 1, p. 10, 2008.

[KIM 12] KIM J.-D., WANG Y., "CSAF – a community-sourcing annotation framework", *Proceedings of the Sixth Linguistic Annotation Workshop*, Association for Computational Linguistics, pp. 153–156, 2012.

[KIN 13] KING D.L., HAAGSMA M.C., DELFABBRO P.H. *et al.*, "Toward a consensus definition of pathological video-gaming: a systematic review of psychometric assessment tools", *Clinical Psychology Review*, vol. 33, no. 3, pp. 331–342, 2013.

[KIT 07] KITTUR A., CHI E., PENDLETON B.A. *et al.*, "Power of the few vs. wisdom of the crowd: Wikipedia and the rise of the bourgeoisie", *World Wide Web*, vol. 1, no. 2, p. 19, 2007.

[KLE 09] KLEBANOV B.B., BEIGMAN E., "From annotator agreement to noise models", *Computational Linguistics*, vol. 35, no. 4, pp. 495–503, 2009.

[KRI 80] KRIPPENDORFF K., *Content Analysis: An Introduction to Its Methodology*, Sage, Beverly Hills, CA, USA, 1980.

[KRI 04] KRIPPENDORFF K., *Content Analysis: An Introduction to Its Methodology*, 2nd ed., Sage, Thousand Oaks, CA., USA, 2004.

[KRI 13] KRIPPENDORFF K., *Content Analysis: An Introduction to Its Methodology*, 3rd ed., Sage, Thousand Oaks, CA, 2013.

[KRU 09] KRUSCHWITZ U., CHAMBERLAIN J., POESIO M., "(Linguistic) Science Through Web Collaboration in the ANAWIKI project", *Proceedings of the WebSci'09: Society On-Line*, 2009.

[LAF 08] LAFOURCADE M., JOUBERT A., "JeuxDeMots: un prototype ludique pour l'émergence de relations entre termes", *Journées internationales d'Analyse statistique des Données Textuelles (JADT)*, Lyon, France, 2008.

[LAF 14] LAFOURCADE M., LEBRUN N., "Éthique et construction collaborative de données lexicales par des GWAPs", *Journée d'étude ATALA Éthique et*, TAL, November 2014.

[LAF 15a] LAFOURCADE M., JOUBERT A., "TOTAKI: A Help for Lexical Access on the TOT Problem", *Language Production, Cognition, and the Lexicon. Festschrift in honor of Michael Zock*, vol. XI of Text, Speech and Language Technology, pp. 95–112, Springer, Dordrecht, 2015.

[LAF 15b] LAFOURCADE M., LE BRUN N., JOUBERT A., "Vous aimez ?...ou pas ? LikeIt, un jeu pour construire une ressource lexicale de polarité", *Actes de la 22e conférence sur le Traitement Automatique des Langues Naturelles*, Caen, France, Association pour le Traitement Automatique des Langues, pp. 330–336, June 2015.

[LAF 15c] LAFOURCADE M., LEBRUN N., JOUBERT A., *Games with a Purpose (GWAPs)*, ISTE Ltd, London, and John Wiley & Sons, New York, 2015.

[LAI 09] LAIGNELET M., RIOULT F., "Repérer automatiquement les segments obsolescents à l'aide d'indices sémantiques et discursifs", *Traitement Automatique des Langues Naturelles (TALN)*, Senlis, France, 2009.

[LAN 77] LANDIS J.R., KOCH G.G., "The measurement of observer agreement for categorical data", *Biometrics*, vol. 33, no. 1, pp. 159–174, International Biometric Society, 1977.

[LAN 12] LANDRAGIN F., POIBEAU T., VICTORRI B., "ANALEC: a new tool for the dynamic annotation of textual data", *International Conference on Language Resources and Evaluation (LREC)*, European Language Resources Association (ELRA), 23–25, May 2012.

[LAT 87] LATOUR B., *Science in Action: How to Follow Scientists and Engineers through Society*,   Harvard University Press, Cambridge, MA, 1987.

[LEB 08] LEBARBÉ T., "CLELIA: Building a Manucript Archive throught Interdisciplinary Dialogue", *The Marriage of Mercury and Philology: Problems and Outcomes in Digital Philology*, 2008.

[LEE 93] LEECH G., "Corpus annotation schemes", *Literary and Linguistic Computing*, vol. 8, no. 4, pp. 275–281, 1993.

[LEE 97] LEECH G., "Corpus annotation: Linguistic information from computer text corpora", *Introducing Corpus Annotation*, pp. 1–18, Longman, 1997.

[LIB 09] LIBERMAN M., "The annotation conundrum", *Proceedings of the EACL 2009 Workshop on the Interaction Between Linguistics and Computational Linguistics: Virtuous, Vicious or Vacuous?*, ILCL '09, Stroudsburg, PA, USA, Association for Computational Linguistics, p. 2, 2009.

[LOR 06] LORTAL G., LEWKOWICZ M., TODIRACU-COURTIER A., "Des activités d'annotation: De la glose au document", in SALEMBIER P., ZACKLAD M. (eds), *Annotations dans les documents pour l'action*, Hermes-Lavoisier, Paris, 2006.

[MAE 04] MAEDA K., STRASSEL S., "Annotation tools for large-scale corpus development: using AGTK at the Linguistic Data Consortium", *International Conference on Language Resources and Evaluation (LREC)*, 2004.

[MAE 06] MAEDA K., LEE H., MEDERO J. *et al.*, "A New Phase in annotation tool development at the linguistic data consortium: the evolution of the Annotation Graph Toolkit", *International Conference on Language Resources and Evaluation (LREC)*, May 2006.

[MAK 99] MAKHOUL J., KUBALA F., SCHWARTZ R. *et al.*, "Performance measures for information extraction", *Proceedings of DARPA Broadcast News Workshop*, pp. 249–252, 1999.

[MAR 93] MARCUS M., SANTORINI B., MARCINKIEWICZ, M.A., "Building a large annotated corpus of English: the Penn Treebank", *Computational Linguistics*, vol. 19, no. 2, pp. 313–330, 1993.

[MAR 15] MARCZEWSKI A., *Even Ninja Monkeys Like to Play: Gamification, Game Thinking and Motivational Design*, CreateSpace Independent Publishing Platform, 1st edition, 2015.

[MAT 11] MATHET Y., WIDLÖCHER A., "Une approche holiste et unifiée de l'alignement et de la mesure d'accord inter-annotateurs", *Traitement Automatique des Langues Naturelles (TALN)*, Montpellier, France, 2011.

[MAT 12] MATHET Y., WIDLÖCHER A., FORT K. *et al.*, "Manual Corpus Annotation: Evaluating the Evaluation Metrics", *International Conference on Computational Linguistics (COLING)*, pp. 809–818, 2012, Poster.

[MAT 15] MATHET Y., WIDLÖCHER A., MÉTIVIER J.-P., "The unified and holistic method gamma (γ) for inter-annotator agreement measure and alignment", *Computational Linguistics*, vol. 41, no. 3, pp. 437–479, 2015.

[MOR 03] MORTON T., LACIVITA J., "WordFreak: an open tool for linguistic annotation", *Proceedings of the 2003 Conference of the North American Chapter of the Association for Computational Linguistics on Human Language Technology: Demonstrations Volume 4*, NAACL-Demonstrations '03, Stroudsburg, PA, USA, Association for Computational Linguistics, pp. 17–18, 2003.

[MÜL 06] MÜLLER C., STRUBE M., "Multi-level annotation of linguistic data with MMAX2", in BRAUN S., KOHN K., MUKHERJEE J. (eds), *Corpus Technology and Language Pedagogy: New Resources, New Tools, New Methods*, pp. 197–214, Peter Lang, 2006.

[MUZ 85] MUZERELLE D., *Vocabulaire codicologique: répertoire méthodique des termes français relatifs aux manuscrits*, Editions CEMI, Paris, 1985.

[NAK 02] NAKAMURA J., CSIKSZENTMIHALYI M., "The concept of flow", *Handbook of Positive Psychology*, pp. 89–105, 2002.

[NÉD 06] NÉDELLEC C., BESSIÈRES P., BOSSY R. *et al.*, "Annotation guidelines for machine learning-based named entity recognition in microbiology", in NÉDELLEC C. (ed.), *Proceedings of the Data and text mining in integrative biology workshop*, pp. 40–54, 2006.

[NOV 10] NOVOTNEY S., CALLISON-BURCH C., "Cheap, fast and good enough: automatic speech recognition with non-expert transcription", *Annual Conference of the North American Chapter of the Association for Computational Linguistics (NAACL)*, HLT'10, Stroudsburg, PA, USA, Association for Computational Linguistics, pp. 207–215, 2010.

[O'D 08] O'DONNELL M., "Demonstration of the UAM CorpusTool for text and image annotation", *Proceedings of the 46th Annual Meeting of the Association for Computational Linguistics on Human Language Technologies: Demo Session*, HLT-Demonstrations '08, Stroudsburg, PA, USA, Association for Computational Linguistics, pp. 13–16, 2008.

[OGR 06] OGREN P., "Knowtator: a plug-in for creating training and evaluation data sets for Biomedical Natural Language systems", *Protégé Conference*, Stanford, USA, 2006.

[ORA 03] ORASAN C., "PALinkA: a highly customisable tool for discourse annotation", *Proceedings of SIGdial Workshop on Discourse and Dialogue*, 2003.

[PAL 05] PALMER M., GILDEA D., KINGSBURY P., "The proposition bank: an annotated corpus of semantic roles", *Computational Linguistics*, vol. 31, pp. 71–106, 2005.

[PÉR 11] PÉRY-WOODLEY M.-P., AFANTENOS S., HO-DAC L.-M. *et al.*, "La ressource ANNODIS, un corpus enrichi d'annotations discursives", *Traitement Automatique des Langues*, vol. 52, no. 3, pp. 71–101, ATALA, 2011.

[PET 12] PETASIS G., "The SYNC3 Collaborative annotation tool", *International Conference on Language Resources and Evaluation (LREC)*, European Language Resources Association (ELRA), 23-25, May 2012.

[PEV 02] PEVZNER L., HEARST M.A., "A critique and improvement of an evaluation metric for text segmentation", *Computational Linguistics*, vol. 28, no. 1, pp. 19–36, MIT Press, March 2002.

[POE 05] POESIO M., ARTSTEIN R., "The reliability of anaphoric annotation, reconsidered: taking ambiguity into account", *Proceedings of the Workshop on Frontiers in Corpus Annotations II: Pie in the Sky*, Ann Arbor, Michigan, USA, Association for Computational Linguistics, pp. 76–83, 2005.

[PRZ 09] PRZEPIÓRKOWSKI A., MURZYNOWSKI G., "Manual annotation of the National Corpus of Polish with Anotatornia", in GOŹDŹ-ROSZKOWSKI S. (ed.), *The Proceedings of Practical Applications in Language and Computers PALC 2009*, Peter Lang, 2009.

[PUS 12] PUSTEJOVSKY J., STUBBS A., *Natural Language Annotation for Machine Learning*, O'Reilly, 2012.

[REI 05] REIDSMA D., JOVANOVIC N., HOFS D., "Designing annotation tools based on properties of annotation problems", *Measuring Behavior 2005, 5th International Conference on Methods and Techniques in Behavioral Research*, August 2005.

[REI 08] REIDSMA D., CARLETTA J., "Reliability measurement without limits", *Computational Linguistics*, vol. 34, no. 3, pp. 319–326, MIT Press, 2008.

[ROS 10] ROSS J., IRANI L., SILBERMAN M.S. *et al.*, "Who are the crowdworkers?: shifting demographics in mechanical turk", *Proceedings of the 28th of the International Conference Extended Abstracts on Human Factors in Computing Systems*, CHI EA '10, New York, USA, ACM, pp. 2863–2872, 2010.

[ROS 12] ROSSET S., GROUIN C., FORT K. *et al.*, "Structured named entities in two distinct press corpora: contemporary broadcast news and old newspapers", *6th Linguistic Annotation Workshop (LAW VI)*, pp. 40–48, 2012.

[SAM 00] SAMPSON G., "The role of taxonomy in language engineering", *Philosophical Transactions of the Royal Society of London, Series A: Mathematical, Physical and Engineering Sciences*, vol. 358, no. 1769, pp. 1339–1355, 2000.

[SAN 90] SANTORINI B., Part-of-speech tagging guidelines for the Penn Treebank Project, Report no. MS-CIS-90-47, Department of Computer and Information Science, University of Pennsylvania, 1990.

[SCH 97] SCHMID H., "New methods in language processing, studies in computational linguistics", *Probabilistic Part-of-Speech Tagging Using Decision Trees*, pp. 154–164, UCL Press, London, 1997.

[SCO 55] SCOTT W.A., "Reliability of content analysis: the case of nominal scale coding", *Public Opinion Quaterly*, vol. 19, no. 3, pp. 321–325, 1955.

[SIE 88] SIEGEL S., CASTELLAN N.J., *Nonparametric Statistics for the Behavioral Sciences*, McGraw-Hill, New York, USA, 2nd edition, 1988.

[SIN 05] SINCLAIR J., *"Developing Linguistic Corpora: a Guide to Good Practice"*, Chapter Corpus and Text – Basic Principles, pp. 1–16, Oxford: Oxbow Books, 2005.

[SNO 08] SNOW R., O'CONNOR B., JURAFSKY D. *et al.*, "Cheap and fast – but is it good? Evaluating non-expert annotations for natural language tasks", *Proceedings of EMNLP 2008*, pp. 254–263, 2008.

[STÜ 07] STÜHRENBERG M., GOECKE D., DIEWALD N. *et al.*, "Web-based annotation of anaphoric relations and lexical chains", *Linguistic Annotation Workshop*, LAW '07, Association for Computational Linguistics, pp. 140–147, 2007.

[STE 11] STENETORP P., TOPIĆ G., PYYSALO S. *et al.*, "BioNLP Shared Task 2011: Supporting Resources", *BioNLP Shared Task 2011 Workshop*, Portland, Oregon, USA, Association for Computational Linguistics, pp. 112–120, 2011.

[STE 12] STENETORP P., PYYSALO S., TOPIĆ G. *et al.*, "brat: a web-based tool for NLP-assisted text annotation", *Proceedings of the Demonstrations at the 13th Conference of the European Chapter of the Association for Computational Linguistics*, Avignon, France, Association for Computational Linguistics, pp. 102–107, April 2012.

[STE 15] STEWART N., UNGEMACH C., HARRIS A.J.L. *et al.*, "The average laboratory samples a population of 7,300 Amazon Mechanical Turk Workers", *Judgment and Decision Making*, vol. 10, no. 10, pp. 479–491, September 2015.

[SWE 05] SWEETSER P., WYETH P., "GameFlow: a model for evaluating player enjoyment in games", *Computers in Entertainment (CIE)*, vol. 3, no. 3, pp. 3, ACM, 2005.

[TEL 14] TELLIER M., "Quelques orientations méthodologiques pour étudier la gestuelle dans des corpus spontanés et semi-contrôlés", *Discours*, vol. 15, 2014.

[URI 13] URIELI A., Robust French syntax analysis: reconciling statistical methods and linguistic knowledge in the Talismane toolkit, PhD thesis, University of Toulouse II le Mirail, France, 2013.

[VÉR 00] VÉRONIS J., "Annotation automatique de corpus: panorama et état de la technique", in PIERREL J.M., *Ingénierie des langues*, Hermes-Lavoisier, 2000.

[VOO 08] VOORMANN H., GUT U., "Agile corpus creation", *Corpus Linguistics and Linguistic Theory*, vol. 4no. 2, pp. 235–251, 2008.

[VOS 05] VOSS J., "Measuring Wikipedia", *Proceedings International Conference of the International Society for Scientometrics and Informetrics ISSI*, Stockholm, Sweden, July 2005.

[WID 09] WIDLÖCHER A., MATHET Y., "La plate-forme Glozz: environnement d'annotation et d'exploration de corpus", *Traitement Automatique des Langues Naturelles (TALN)*, Senlis, France, 2009.

[WOL 11] WOLIŃSKI M., GŁOWIŃSKA K., ŚWIDZIŃSKI M., "A Preliminary Version of Składnica – a Treebank of Polish", *Proceedings of the 5th Language and Technology Conference*, 2011.

[WYN 05] WYNNE M. (ed.), *Developing Linguistic Corpora: a Guide to Good Practice*, Oxbow Books, Oxford, 2005.

Index

Other titles from

in

Cognitive Science and Knowledge Management

2016

GIANNI Robert
Responsibility and Freedom
(Responsible Research and Innovation Set – Volume 2)

LENOIR Virgil Cristian
Ethical Efficiency: Responsibility and Contingency
(Responsible Research and Innovation Set – Volume 1)

MATTA Nada, ATIFI Hassan, DUCELLIER Guillaume
Daily Knowledge Valuation in Organizations

NOUVEL Damien, EHRMANN Maud, ROSSET Sophie
Named Entities for Computational Linguistics

SILBERZTEIN Max
Formalizing Natural Languages: The NooJ Approach

2015

LAFOURCADE Mathieu, JOUBERT Alain, LE BRUN Nathalie
Games with a Purpose (GWAPs)

SAAD Inès, ROSENTHAL-SABROUX Camille, GARGOURI Faïez
Information Systems for Knowledge Management

2014

DELPECH Estelle Maryline
Comparable Corpora and Computer-assisted Translation

FARINAS DEL CERRO Luis, INOUE Katsumi
Logical Modeling of Biological Systems

MACHADO Carolina, DAVIM J. Paulo
Transfer and Management of Knowledge

TORRES-MORENO Juan-Manuel
Automatic Text Summarization

2013

TURENNE Nicolas
Knowledge Needs and Information Extraction: Towards an Artificial Consciousness

ZARATÉ Pascale
Tools for Collaborative Decision-Making

2011

DAVID Amos
Competitive Intelligence and Decision Problems

LÉVY Pierre
The Semantic Sphere: Computation, Cognition and Information Economy

LIGOZAT Gérard
Qualitative Spatial and Temporal Reasoning

PELACHAUD Catherine
Emotion-oriented Systems

QUONIAM Luc
Competitive Intelligence 2.0: Organization, Innovation and Territory

2010

ALBALATE Amparo, MINKER Wolfgang
Semi-Supervised and Unsupervised Machine Learning: Novel Strategies

BROSSAUD Claire, REBER Bernard
Digital Cognitive Technologies

2009

BOUYSSOU Denis, DUBOIS Didier, PIRLOT Marc, PRADE Henri
Decision-making Process

MARCHAL Alain
From Speech Physiology to Linguistic Phonetics

PRALET Cédric, SCHIEX Thomas, VERFAILLIE Gérard
Sequential Decision-Making Problems / Representation and Solution

SZÜCSAndras, TAIT Alan, VIDAL Martine, BERNATH Ulrich
Distance and E-learning in Transition

2008

MARIANI Joseph
Spoken Language Processing